© 1999, revised edition 2020, Harrie Salman

Authorized translation of "Die Soziale Welt als Mysterienstätte",
Lazarus Verlag, Raisdorf, Germany, 1994

Harrie Salman

The Social World As Mystery Center

All rights reserved. No part of this publication may be reproduced, stored in a retrieval system or transmited in any form or by any means, electronic, mechanical, photocopying, recording or otherwise without the prior permision of the author or publisher.

Published by Threefold Publishing
PO Box 251, Mountlake Terrace, WA 98043

Translated by Helga Schulte-Schroer

English Edition Edited by Elizabeth Simons

Designed by Anne Nicholson

A CIP record for this book is available from the Library of Congress Cataloging-in-Publication Data

ISBN: 978-1-7923-2439-0

Printed and bound in United States of America

HARRIE SALMAN

# The Social World As Mystery Center
## The Social Vision of Anthroposophy

HARRIE SALMAN

# The Social World As Mystery Center

## The Social Vision of Anthroposophy

# CONTENTS

THE UNKNOWN ARCHANGEL . . . . . . . . . . . . . . . . . . . . . 1
PROLOGUE . . . . . . . . . . . . . . . . . . . . . . . . . . . . . . . . . . . . . 3
INTRODUCTION . . . . . . . . . . . . . . . . . . . . . . . . . . . . . . . . 9
Chapter I: RUDOLF STEINER
    1. Central Europe as Spiritual Home . . . . . . . . . . . . 13
    2. The Social Question . . . . . . . . . . . . . . . . . . . . . . . . 15
    3. Rudolf Steiner as Philosopher of Freedom . . . . . 17
    4. Rudolf Steiner and Theosophy . . . . . . . . . . . . . . . 20
Chapter II: THE ANTHROPOSOPHICAL SOCIAL IMPULSE
    1. What is Social? . . . . . . . . . . . . . . . . . . . . . . . . . . . . 25
    2. The Social Impulse in Rudolf Steiner's Life . . . . . 28
    3. The Fundamental Sociological Law . . . . . . . . . . . 31
    4. The Fundamental Social Law . . . . . . . . . . . . . . . . 32
    5. The Archetypal Phenomenon of Social Life . . . . 36
    6. Social Threefolding . . . . . . . . . . . . . . . . . . . . . . . . 40
    7. Rudolf Steiner as Social Person . . . . . . . . . . . . . . 54
Chapter III: FROM OLD TO NEW MYSTERIES
    1. A Revolution in Spiritual Life . . . . . . . . . . . . . . . . 60
    2. The Path to the New Mysteries . . . . . . . . . . . . . . . 68
    3. Awakening "on" and "in" the Other . . . . . . . . . . . 75
    4. The Destiny of the Society . . . . . . . . . . . . . . . . . . 91
    5. Rudolf Steiner's Path of the Cross . . . . . . . . . . . . 103

Chapter IV: THE SOCIAL WORLD AS MYSTERY CENTER
    1. The Long Way Towards Summer.............107
    2. The Spiritual World Opens .................112
    3. Daily Life as Mystery Drama................117
    4. Learning to Cooperate ....................127
    5. The Path of Social Development.............137
Chapter V: THE CREATION OF COMMUNITIES
    1. Community building......................151
    2. Culture Islands...........................161
    3. The Social Intentions of Rudolf Steiner.......168
    4. The Rebirth of Anthroposophy..............171
    5. The Anthroposophical Society .............177
    6. A Model for the Future ...................184
EPILOGUE: AWAKENING TO A NEW ERA ..........191

*Motto for new social ethics:*

It is healing only, when
in the mirror of the soul of man
the whole community forms itself;
and in the community
lives the strength of the individual soul.

*Rudolf Steiner (for Edith Maryon,
Wahrspruchworte 1920)*


In the name of the Eternal, the God of Israel:
May Michael be on my right side,
Gabriel on my left side,
Uriel before me,
Raphael behind me
and by my head God's Majesty.

*A Jewish night prayer*

# THE UNKNOWN ARCHANGEL

The cover of this book shows a fresco from the Church of the Transfiguration of the Redeemer on Elijah Street, Novgorod (North Russia). It was painted by Theophanes the Greek in 1378 and portrays the Archangel Uriel. His name means "Light" or "Flame of God", and he is one of the four sublime angels whom God placed around his throne to guide the development of the world. Michael, Gabriel and Raphael are the other three.

Uriel does not appear in the Biblical canon. He is considered the cherub with the fiery sword from the third chapter of Genesis who guards, at the Gates of Eden, the access to the Tree of Life. In the apocryphal Book of Enoch, God sends Uriel to Noah to warn him of the upcoming great flood and to instruct him to build the Ark. In other traditions such as the Kabbalah, Uriel is a Seraph, the Regent of the Sun, the Angel of the Holy Spirit, the Guard over the Realm of the Dead, the Archangel of Salvation. Depictions of Uriel are rare in Christian art, usually showing him with a sword, a staff, a flame, a lantern or a bowl of incense.

Rudolf Steiner described in his *St. John Imagination* how Uriel appears as shining intelligence in the summertime.[1] He is active in the light, evoking the image of the Trinity. His reddish warm coun-

---
[1] Rudolf Steiner: *Das Miterleben des Jahreslaufes in vier kosmischen Imaginationen* (1923), Dornach 1989 (CW 229).

tenance has the serious, judging gaze placed on human misdeeds. His arm-like wings form an admonishing gesture, calling people to transform their misdeeds into virtues.

According to Steiner, Uriel played a leading role in the first stage of the development of our planetary system (in spiritual science called Old Saturn), as did Raphael in the second one (Old Sun), Gabriel in the third (Old Moon), and Michael in the present Earth evolution.[2] The Archangel Oriphiel is known in spiritual science as ruler of Saturn. Oriphiel, the angel of divine wrath, represents the level of archangel-activity of Uriel whose actual rank in the hierarchy of angels lies much higher. The admonishing gesture of Uriel appears when we associate with others in social life. He brings us to self-judgment so that we will work on ourselves and develop the necessary social qualities. The path of social development described in this book is the Urielic path. Uriel is the inspirer of the new professions rooted in the social impulse, and of the sacramentalization of professional life and life in general.

We have to discover the qualities of Uriel when we want to renew culture. He is the unknown archangel. He looks to modern spiritual movements and encourages human beings who want to be inspired by spiritual insights and associate with one another on the basis of a social impulse. We are in need of Uriel's help for the humanization of social life and the creation of new social forms in which modern spiritual consciousness can contribute to a new culture.

Harrie Salman
Noordwijk, Holland

---

[2] Rudolf Steiner: *Freemasonry and Ritual Work*, Great Barrington 2007. In the German edition p. 336 (CW 265).

# PROLOGUE

In the early hours of January 1, 1923 the Dutch physician Ita Wegman (1876-1943) stood next to Rudolf Steiner (1861-1925), the inaugurator of the spiritual science of Anthroposophy, while the first Goetheanum burned to the ground.[3] A picture of Steiner as she had never seen him before arose in her during this dramatic event. She saw that he, who had always been there for others, was standing very alone. Since then Wegman carried this picture in her soul and decided to put herself entirely at the service of his mission.

Out of this union of souls, a question germinated in her that gave him the opportunity to initiate a renewal of spiritual life. This was a question concerning new mysteries, new ways to consciously connect with the spiritual world. This question is relevant for everybody now. Rudolf Steiner developed a new vision that shows how we can become conscious creators of a new social life and a new culture. This vision is still hardly recognized in its universal importance. It is to the credit of Dieter Brüll, an expert on fiscal law and social questions, to have shown in his book *The Mysteries of Social Encounters – The Anthroposophical Social Impulse*, originally published in 1984, how this vision came to unfold in Steiner's life.[4]

---

[3] The Goetheanum is the center of the anthroposophical movement in Dornach, near Basle in Switzerland.

[4] Dieter Brüll: *The Mysteries of Social Encounters - The Anthroposophical Social Impulse*, Fair Oaks 2002.

This vision makes it clear that spiritual experiences and insights are not only a personal matter, but can also arise in encounters and cooperation with others. In our present era we can be inspired by spiritual beings in social life. The places where individuals used to receive such inspirations are called "mystery centers". In the cultures of Antiquity these were temple complexes and other holy places. Preparation for contact with spiritual beings took place through initiation, in which organs of supersensible perception were opened that in ancient India were called chakras.

For centuries there were no more places of initiation in Europe, but since the beginning of the 20th century it has been possible again to communicate with spiritual beings. This can happen in a conscious way, not only in meditation but also in social life. Thus the social world itself becomes a mystery center. This requires a new awareness of the connection of spiritual and social life. The awakening of this awareness was the goal of a renewal process that Steiner wanted to initiate during the important conference at Christmastime in 1923-24, at which time the Anthroposophical Society was re-established. In doing so, he opened up the perspective of working together on a spiritual culture based on a conscious relationship with the spiritual world. This work needs the support of a new social life and the creation of communities.

Steiner expected that millions of people would connect with this renewal movement and that at the end of the 20th century a certain culmination of Anthroposophical work would be reached. During the aforementioned conference he therefore called on the members of the Anthroposophical Society, who had problems with each other, to work together. However, this did not happen, and as a result this conference had failed for him. Steiner died already in 1925, and the General Anthroposophical Society fell apart in 1935. In 1960 most of the conflicts were settled, but Anthroposophy was only to some extent able to fulfil its role as a cultural factor and to spiritualize our way of thinking in all areas of life. Nevertheless, millions of people became acquainted with Waldorf pedagogy, Anthroposophical medicine, biodynamic agriculture and other cultural innovations resulting from Anthroposophy.

Work on a spiritual culture continues in our time also by people who have no connection with the General Anthroposophical Society. This Society, which in 2017 had around 45,000 members worldwide, faces the challenge of renewing itself in such a way that it can fulfil its assigned role in the renewal of culture. This involves learning from the past and discovering the significance of the social impulse of Anthroposophy, which was not understood a century ago.

In recent decades new professions have been developing that connect spiritual and social impulses. They are social, therapeutic and artistic professions that, in the first place, help support people on their individual path of development, make the threads and knots of their destiny visible and help them accept their life's challenges. And secondly, support people who want to realize new forms of association and cooperation with others as well as new social structures in their social environment. These new professions are concerned with uniting people with their destiny, ordering destiny that has come into disarray, regenerating life forces, rebalancing soul forces, structuring organizations, solving conflicts and healing social relationships. Developments in the fields of biography work, counseling, artistic therapies, social threefolding and organization consultancy are the first beginnings of these new spheres of work. In line with this lies a new way of dealing with money, labor and land, a just order of the world and a moral use of technology.

Since 1971 my path through Anthroposophy led me from old to new mysteries. It began with Rudolf Steiner's book, *Christianity as Mystical Fact* and the *Mysteries of Antiquity,* which I discovered while exploring the Greek and Egyptian mysteries. Over the years

I began to perceive how new mysteries are enacted between people in everyday life.

The first version of this book was written in 1992 in the Dutch language, with the title *Het beeld van de ander* [The Image of the Other Person]. After the publication of the German edition in 1994, it was translated by enthusiastic readers into Czech, English, Hebrew and Russian. The English edition, published in 1999, is still widely read, and for this reason a revised edition appears after 21 years. The first edition was written for people connected with Anthroposophy who were looking for the regeneration of the Anthroposophical impulses. This new edition aims at a larger readership that is interested in Rudolf Steiner's social ideas. His thoughts on community building as a path towards a conscious connection with the spiritual world are still highly relevant.

These thoughts are in fact relevant for everybody. Anthroposophy is a new spiritual impulse for humanity, an impulse that is larger than what has come to life in the Anthroposophical world. It is a new form of consciousness about who we are as human beings and how we can realize our spiritual potential. For a century, Anthroposophy has lived as an impulse in the higher consciousness of all people, but a language that can be understood by every present-day human being and an openness to the spiritual world are necessary to bring it down into daily consciousness.

A new spirituality needs time to develop and it needs appropriate social forms to manifest itself in initiatives, groups and institutions. Rudolf Steiner created a social vision to make this possible, but that was not properly understood a century ago. This vision is oriented towards the future of a humanity that wants to once more connect with spiritual beings and apply their inspirations in social life.

The renewal of culture begins on a small scale, in the family, in education, in a conscious way of living, eating, dealing with our health and nature, and in discovering the spiritual dimensions of life. On a larger scale, it is about transforming our materialistic culture into a spiritual culture and about creating a humane society that treats the earth responsibly. What started a century ago as an impulse for renewal, and from the 1960s onwards has moved youth around the world, is now returning in our age of social inequality, global refugee flows, climate change and epidemics as tasks which no one can neglect.

As a Dutchman I would like to make some remarks about the role of Dutch Anthroposophy in this process of renewal. Ever since the late Middle Ages, the inhabitants of the western part of the country, which lies below sea level, have been forced to work together to take care of the dikes. The protection of the low lands gave rise to a model of cooperation, in which all relevant people can participate and decide in consultations. In this way, the reclamation of physical land has transformed into the building of new land in social life. This might be regarded as a special mission of the Netherlands. In social life we work with etheric forces, we connect people's life energies.

This forms the historical background of the work for social threefolding in the Netherlands, which was developed by many Anthroposophists, among them Dieter Brüll, the author of the book on the Anthroposophical Social Impulse. We also see this mission in the work of the NPI Institute for Organizational Development, founded in 1954 by Bernard Lievegoed together with a circle of organizational advisors, and in the work of the prominent NPI staff members Lex Bos, author of books dealing with social problems, and Adriaan Bekman, in 2005 founder of the IMO, the International Institute for Human and Organizational Development.

The Dutch Anthroposophical Society is also aware that in social life we are building new land in the etheric. The focus of the work of its board is "etheric organising": supporting people with their initiatives and connecting these initiatives with each other. It is an art to create together the substance and the temporary forms that fit the active formative power of an initiative. This modelling and transforming of social forms is a social art that needs to be practiced continuously. The centre of the Society is not the board, but the initiatives of its members. In this way the intentions that Rudolf Steiner connected with working on a new culture in 1923 become visible again.

The starting point for this work is the initiative community of active people who meet each other in inspiring member groups. This is the Anthroposophical Society that Steiner wanted to establish in 1923, but which disappeared from the consciousness of its members after his death. A community of initiators needs the support from a board that takes on the facilitating tasks that Steiner wanted to place in the General Anthroposophical Society. Due to a lack of awareness, the latter Society also took over the tasks of the first Society, while Steiner wanted to differentiate their tasks. As the third part of his threefold vision, Steiner saw his School for Spiritual Science, a workshop for connecting with the spiritual world in new mysteries. It is my conviction that this original threefold social structure is necessary for the spiritual work of the future.

# INTRODUCTION

This book is concerned with the Anthroposophical Social Impulse and Rudolf Steiner's intentions with it. He foresaw that from the middle of the 20th century onwards the processes of social disintegration would speed up. In the meantime, we can see how social traditions are losing their strength. It is becoming increasingly difficult to live with each other without conflict. New forms of community building are necessary, as well as a new spiritual culture to counter the growing social isolation and materialism. Steiner saw the need for new, healthy social conditions in society and for a spiritual revolution within traditional spiritual life. This revolution was to lead to new mysteries as a source of a new spiritual culture.

The 20th century was a most dramatic century, in which the course of history changed completely. Steiner was totally shocked when the First World War broke out in 1914. He knew that it was being prepared, but he thought that it would begin later. His project of spiritual renewal was in danger. This war led to the collapse of Central Europe, and indirectly to the rise of Nazism in 1933. The Second World War led to the decline of European culture and the incorporation of Western Europe in the American World Order.

An economic, scientific and technological development began that overwhelmed humanity with effective forms of consciousness manipulation. While Rudolf Steiner opened the gate to the spiritual world and announced the Second Coming of Christ, his opponents opened the gate to the subconscious world and awoke the dark forces that are connected with the Antichrist. Steiner had expected that he would live into the 1940s, but he had to leave his earthly body in 1925.

To enable a new blossoming of Anthroposophy, we have to contemplate Steiner's spiritual and social intentions. When we do this, it is good to realize that young people today have another connection with the spiritual world than the older generations for whom this relationship was still mediated by a church or by an institution such as the Anthroposophical Society. The spiritual life of the younger generations is much more personal, and for many it is limited to a search for the meaning of life in a world of technology that continually lures our consciousness into new prisons of manipulation and addiction.

Rudolf Steiner was able to speak freely about Christ in his time. This is no longer a matter of course for many people who have no connection with the traditional churches. For Steiner, Christ is greater than Christianity. He is there for all mankind. Steiner spoke of him as the Spirit of the Sun and called him an avatar. Those who have seen the film *Avatar* are familiar with this concept. It comes from Hinduism and it refers to a high spiritual being who can work through a highly developed human being. For Steiner, Christ was the highest spiritual being who connected with the highly developed man Jesus to bring a mission of love among mankind and to reconnect people with their higher Self. When Steiner spoke of the Christ impulse, he meant the impulse of love.

The first chapter of this book presents a picture of Rudolf Steiner as a human being in the culture and society of his time. As a philosopher of freedom he devoted himself at the beginning of the 20th century to the spiritual development of the proletariat in Berlin.

At the same time he lectured in the German Theosophical movement as an authority on Christian spirituality. The second chapter describes the Anthroposophical Social Impulse. The third chapter is about the transformation of an old spiritual consciousness into a new spirituality in which a conscious connection with the world of the spirit becomes possible. The fourth chapter clarifies the vision of the social world having become a mystery center in which the spirit is directly active between people. We enter a new stage of consciousness where we can have spiritual experiences in social life and can experience and understand everything that happens in social life as spiritual reality. The fifth chapter asks how modern spiritual consciousness can lead to the creation of a new communities in which people can develop spiritually inspired initiatives. The General Anthroposophical Society can support this process and connect them.

CHAPTER I

# RUDOLF STEINER

## 1. Central Europe as Spiritual Home

Spiritual movements need a channel, a stream in which they can flow. At the beginning of the 20th century Central European culture provided a channel for Anthroposophy. It was alive with a spirituality based on the freedom of each individual, and an image of humanity that distinguished between body, soul and spirit. It had a social component as well, since the Central European consciousness of freedom had developed the social forms necessary for its full unfolding. It was part of an order of freedom that inspired people to create their social life out of their consciousness of rights.

In its development through a millennium, Central Europe had been the spiritual home of a great variety of spiritual streams like

Rosicrucianism, the Czech Hussites, German Protestantism, Romanticism and Idealist Philosophy. Movements developing new social forms, as in the medieval free cities, the Swiss Confederation and the Dutch Republic were closely related to them. A spirit of freedom was very much alive, trying to overcome the old principles of power and providing the possibility for a new political life based on the equality of free human beings.

In the early 20th century the spiritual heritage of Romantic and Idealistic times, as well as esoteric Christianity, still lived in the souls of many. When the Austrian philosopher Rudolf Steiner founded a new spiritual science he was able to connect to this heritage. His Anthroposophy embraced the entire Central European culture and renewed it by offering a path of inner development to everyone willing to become creative and develop soul and spirit. This creative activity had earlier been the privilege of genius. However, it was hardly possible for Steiner to connect to the social tradition of Central Europe. The consciousness of freedom and the social radicalism of the earlier Central Europeans had already vanished in the German bourgeoisie of his time.

In the 20th century the spiritual heritage of Central Europe dissociated itself from its geographical context and became global. Everywhere on earth free people discover that Central European consciousness, and Anthroposophy in particular, represent a new stage in the general spiritual development of mankind, and that this consciousness unfolds where spiritually open-minded people pursue spiritual interests. Islands of culture arise once they are able to develop new social forms where the fount of a new spiritual consciousness can renew the social and spiritual life of our time.

Creating a new spiritual culture, a way of life in which we overcome the materialism of our time, is a difficult task, but in small and larger communities this has already begun. In every community we must consciously shape a social life in which we, as free people, organize our cultural, political and economic conditions. The Central European tradition points to a social circle in which all are equal and have the same rights and duties. It is the idea of the forum of citizens, the Round Table, where all take part in political life.

Rudolf Steiner is the pioneer of a new spiritual culture. He loosened Central European culture from the background in which it had developed, and presented it as a level of consciousness of free individuality that every human being can experience in his inner development towards full humanity. Anthroposophy is the clearest expression of this new spiritual consciousness which since the 1960s has awakened in many people all over the world. People engaged in this cultural renewal can observe how Steiner came to understand the social question, and how he transformed old forms of spirituality. Steiner also tried to create communities with appropriate social forms for a new living spirituality. This work must be continued with full commitment to the deep social changes that are necessary in our times.

## 2. The Social Question

The second half of the 19th century saw a radical transformation of European culture and social life. Western influence increased in strength and continues to do so into our time. After the Iron Curtain broke down in 1989, a new wave of Westernizing engulfed the countries of Central and Eastern Europe. Social science describes this process as modernization and regards Western society as an exemplary model of development for global social transformation. Social changes are, however, always connected to conflicts between a main stream leading to a modern society and undercurrents trying to create a different society.

A modern society is a society in which the areas of culture, politics and economics became independent and developed very distinct features. Culture freed itself from the power of traditions. Religion became a private affair, art lost its sacral dimension, and science is limited to researching only the material aspects of reality. A bureaucratic state apparatus settled in the political sphere, only marginally controlled by a parliamentary democracy. Modern economy is a capitalist market economy with technology to provide constant growth. On a global scale, this form of modernization has had disastrous consequences.

The rise of modern society in Central Europe meant the disintegration of traditional community, especially in the industrial areas. Traditional forms of life were destroyed, and individuals knowing themselves to be safe in many cultural, political and economic associations (for example guilds, family associations and church congregations), lost their connection to others and were caught in a web of impersonal conditions. The so-called "Social Question" expresses itself in the dissolution of ties between individual and community. It appears where traditional communities disintegrate, and poses the task of re-creating the social order in a new, conscious way.

Industrial development pulled millions of Central Europeans from the countryside into cities. They became proletarians who had no inner connection to bourgeois culture. Culture was merely ideology to them, something that could not satisfy their spiritual needs. Individuals felt violated in their dignity because they had to sell themselves and their labor on the labor market. There were no traditional associations of mutual help in the city as there had been in the protecting structure of the village, and traditions of folk culture were lost to them as well.

## 3. Steiner as Philosopher of Freedom

Rudolf Steiner was born in 1861 in Kraljevec [Kralyevets], a small village (now in Croatia) in the Austro-Hungarian Empire. In 1879 he matriculated at the Technical University of Vienna. He chose Mathematics, Physics, Biology, Chemistry and German Literature as his subjects. A few years later he met an unknown Master who decisively inspired his path of spiritual development and gave him important advice on the realization of his life's task. This master was, according to a statement from Steiner to the German Christian Community priest Friedrich Rittelmeyer, a reincarnation of Christian Rosenkreutz. He advised Steiner to go the path to the spirit through natural-scientific thinking. Steiner told Rittelmeyer that a second master (Master Jesus, Zarathustra) made him aware of the German philosopher Fichte and his philosophy of the I-consciousness.[5] In this way Steiner was able to know materialism from the inside out and deepen his philosophical thoughts with Fichte's philosophy.

During his studies and later as publisher of Goethe's natural-scientific works, Steiner paid attention to the political events in Austro-Hungary, this state of many ethnic groups, where the question of nationalities became ever more threatening. He also moved in Vienna's literary and scientific circles as described in his autobiography *The Course of My Life*.[6]

When Steiner began his work in the Goethe archives in Weimar in Germany in 1890, he entered a sphere of life strongly oriented to the past. But he also had the opportunity to absorb the works of two people who radically opposed bourgeois traditions and ideas: the natural scientist Ernst Haeckel and the philosopher Friedrich Nietzsche. Steiner crawled, so to speak, into the skin

---

5   Friedrich Rittelmeyer, *Meine Gespräche mit Rudolf Steiner*, Stuttgart 2017, p. 31.

6   Rudolf Steiner: *The Course of My Life* (1923-1925), Hudson 1986 (CW 28).

of their materialistic thought world to find points of contact for a spiritual teaching of evolution and a spiritual image of the human being. At this time he wrote philosophical works such as The Philosophy of Freedom, where he opened the portal of supersensible cognition and created the foundation of moral individualism.[7] In these ethics, human activity is determined by each individual's moral intuition, no longer by natural laws or ethical norms. These moral intuitions enable us to act freely out of cognition of what is good in a given situation without interfering in the free activities of others.

Steiner did not become an academic Goethe specialist. In 1897, his path led to Berlin, where he became editor of a literary magazine. He was in contact with a world of artists, bohemians and other social outsiders, and shared the life and poverty of these homeless people at the edge of a burgeoning modern industrial society. Steiner published and lectured on a variety of topics. He wrote about the emancipation of women, took a stand against French anti-Semitism in the Dreyfuss affair, and was also very critical of Zionism. He was always concerned about freeing the individual from the forceful power of old social forms like church, tradition, nationalism, state, and capitalism.

In a review, Steiner also wrote about the social question. He formulated the Fundamental Sociological Law, describing how in the beginning of culture humanity formed associations in which the interests of the individual were at first sacrificed to those of the associations but that further development led to the freeing of the individual from the interests of the associations and to the free unfolding of the needs and forces of the individual.

To Steiner the state was not a means in itself, but should allow individuals to come to their greatest possible development; the absence of rulership was his ideal. Supporting the emancipation of the individual, he remarked that all individualities would be

---

[7] Rudolf Steiner: *The Philosophy of Spiritual Activity* (1894), Hudson 1986 (CW 4).

suppressed when the ideals of social democracy (that wanted to use state power to create a just society) are realized. State socialism opposes the Fundamental Sociological Law and, Steiner wrote in 1898: "the political system sought by social democracy is the worst rulership of all."[8]

Within the German political context of his day, Steiner formulated his philosophy of freedom as a non-violent individualistic anarchism. He wrote in a letter to his friend John Mackay in 1898:

> The individualistic anarchist does not want to hinder a person to unfold his abilities and forces. The present government is founded on violence and authority; it hates the individual and hinders his free development.[9]

Here we see Steiner as an outspoken representative of the undercurrent of European culture that was devoted to the ideals of freedom within the declining culture of Central Europe. He moved in circles where this stream was still alive. This led him to follow a request by Wilhelm Liebknecht, the leader of the social democratic Workers' Education School in Berlin, to give a course at this school. It was a course held in the spring of 1899 on modern history in relation to spiritual life. Steiner was free to speak out of his own world view, and he gained the trust of the workers. Later he gave other courses on history, natural science and speaker's courses. In 1900 he was asked to give a speech for thousands of typesetters and printers commemorating Gutenberg, the German inventor of printing.

The social democratic leaders did not like these successes. In 1904 they wanted to banish Steiner from the school, but the vast majority of students wanted to keep the popular lecturer. In January of 1905 Steiner decided to leave the school, since he could no longer work in an acceptable way. One of the proletarian leaders, at

---

8  Rudolf Steiner: *Gesammelte Aufsätze zur Kultur- und Zeitgeschichte* (1887-1901), Dornach 1989 (CW 31).

9  Ibid.

the meeting at which he was to be dismissed, emphatically stated: "We do not want freedom in the proletarian movement, we want reasonable force." It was clear to Steiner that the development of the free individual was not wanted at the school.

In his time Steiner was one of a few European intellectuals who, out of a deep interest, was occupied with the spiritual needs and the longing for knowledge of the proletariat in European cities. The workers rejected bourgeois culture, but received superficial materialistic ideas from their leaders instead.

## 4. Steiner and Theosophy

Artists and workers were not the only ones who stood at the periphery of society at the end of the 19th century. Other spiritually homeless groups were more connected with the undercurrents of culture than the main stream of modernization. The unrest in large circles of young people was a peculiar phenomenon. A youth movement arose out of a longing for originality and a connection to nature and human community.

Older people, often from higher circles of society, also longed for spirituality and inner development. Among them were members of the Theosophical Society that had existed in Germany since 1884, and which was founded in 1875 in the United States. Its goal was to form a nucleus of general human brotherhood, to cultivate the seed of truth in all religions and to study the deeper spiritual forces in humanity and the world. But soon a one-sided Buddhist-Hindu stream appeared that allied itself with Anglo-American culture.

Count Brockdorff, the leader of the Berlin Lodge of this Society, invited Rudolf Steiner to the Theosophical Library in 1900. There Steiner gave a lecture on the philosopher Nietzsche. Then, because he met with much approval, he was asked to give a second lecture on Goethe. Steiner clearly stated to the theosophical leaders at that time that he would only speak about the fruits of his own spiritual research. It was known in theosophical circles that he was critical of Eastern-oriented Theosophy. Cycles of lectures on the development of mysticism in European culture and Christianity and the mysteries of Antiquity now followed. Decisive for further cooperation with the Theosophical Society was Steiner's meeting with theosophist Marie von Sivers (1867-1948), who asked him if it was possible to develop a spirituality that would be as deep as Eastern spirituality but have European and Christian foundations. Thanks to her question and her support, Anthroposophy has come into the world. As a result of their meeting, Steiner was invited in 1902 to become the General Secretary of the German section of the Theosophical Society while still a lecturer at the Workers' Education School. At the same time, Steiner presented his own spiritual stream called "Anthroposophy" in lectures to other groups.

Anthroposophy stood in the European-Christian tradition, and most of the German theosophists wanted to unite with it more deeply. However, Christ's central importance for the history of the world was not recognized within the Theosophical Society, He was only seen as one of the great world teachers. From 1909 on, leaders of the Theosophical Society even claimed that Christ would be born again in a young Hindu, later known as Krishnamurti. Steiner had to object strongly to this claim, because earlier in his Berlin years he had his own experience of the mystery of Golgotha (the death and resurrection of Christ). He learned from his clairvoyant observations that the reappearance of Christ would take place on a higher plane than the physical, namely the etheric. It was the beginning of a conflict with Theosophy that finally ended with the exclusion of most of the German theosophists and the founding of the Anthroposophical Society in 1913, which began with around 3,000 members. Steiner worked in this Society only as teacher, without becoming a member himself.

He considered the formulation of the old teaching of karma (destiny) and reincarnation (rebirth) in the context of modern culture and Christianity to be his actual life's task. In 1902 he wanted to start in the Theosophical Society with practical karma exercises. Through these exercises we can gain insight into our destiny and destined relationships with others. However, the directness and relation to one's own personality caused resistance. Steiner had to wait until 1924 before he could speak of it again. The social question also proved to be too concrete for the theosophists. In three essays from 1905 and 1906 (which will be referred to later), Steiner gave an introduction to this question. Not finding any response, the series was discontinued. Neither the bourgeois world nor the theosophical elite had any interest in the proletarian world he had actively worked in for five years.

Rudolf Steiner's connection to the old stream of Theosophy posed the task of re-creating this stream in such a way that it could become a channel for a new spirituality. The German Theosophical Society had been a closed circle guarding esoteric knowledge and its members wanted to develop spiritually under the personal leadership of a teacher. A cult around hidden Masters sending important messages from Tibet and the Himalayans existed there, along with a tendency to escape individual and social reality.

Steiner, on the other hand, envisioned an open society bringing spiritual knowledge to the public and making it encountered in a practical way. He wanted to develop a new spirituality based upon the clear, objective thinking of natural science, and emphasized personal responsibility in activating our inner teacher. Each person was to go his own path of training, to be realized in everyday life, and lay the foundations for a new spiritual culture. Modern times ask us to consciously search for new social forms in which a new spirituality can be active. That spiritual and social life cannot develop independently from each other was understood only by a few, and so the belief arose that if only individual development was brought far enough, the social element would come of itself.

This chapter outlined the framework in which Steiner had developed his ideas on the renewal of social life. These ideas will be elaborated in the next chapter.

CHAPTER II

# THE ANTHROPOSOPHICAL SOCIAL IMPULSE

## 1. What is Social?

Rudolf Steiner posed this radical question: "How do we become social?" He did not mean 'social' in the ordinary sense of the word, as in societal. 'Social' has a much deeper, moral level of meaning connected to our inner life.

In modern society we move in many associations, much more so than in traditional society. We are socialized, we become social beings and we learn how to behave in an adjusted way. Traditions used to guide our development as members of a community and this was supported by our social instincts. However, these inner and outer means of support have been falling away since the second half of the 20th century. Individualism has become stronger and for many it is becoming increasingly difficult to adjust to the norms of society. Modern institutions seem to need disciplined force. Discipline has taken the place of traditions and inborn social instincts since the 18th century, and is forcing us more decisively to be social. In the process, the state with its institutions is becoming the all-mighty controller of social life.

As traditions and social instincts weaken, people increasingly try to exert power over others, and to use others to serve their needs. Many people want to make themselves unassailable and invulnerable, and they retreat to private islands. Communication becomes problematic. We want to meet and understand each other, but it becomes more difficult to create true human relationships. However, a social impulse lives deep within, and Steiner wanted to address this impulse. He pointed to our personality and our ego, which has increased in strength over the last centuries. With all the inner and outer impediments that have fallen away since the middle of the 20th century, our ego now comes to full expression.

Rudolf Steiner considered it part of our natural development to become more and more antisocial. Modern capitalist society with its uninhibited egoism is an expression of this tendency, and can be understood in this sense. This egoism will ultimately lead to a war of all against all if it is not checked. This vision comes from a book written by the English philosopher Thomas Hobbes in 1642. However, our culture also contains forces that want to bring a socially oriented way of life to development, in which people can live together in a brotherly way. Not as ego over ego, but on the level of their higher being.

Steiner spoke out of this deep social impulse and criticized the modern world from this position, thereby expressing his radical individualism. At the same time, he showed ways of developing a new social life on the basis of spiritual knowledge in which our social impulse can become active. It is an impulse to make room for the other inwardly in our soul and outwardly in social forms. Then the other's needs may be experienced so that we can care about them in full consciousness and freedom. With this social impulse the voice of our heart finds expression in our deeds; it is a universal-human voice showing our social attitude of wanting to unite with others.

This place for the other vanishes in the everyday life of modern society. Our ego fills the space in the inter-human sphere. Power structures on higher levels prevent a functioning sphere of rights. It need not surprise us then that Steiner remarked on December 12, 1918, that we are social only when we are sleeping; it is then that we are united with everyone in the spiritual world without being conscious of it. In our normal day consciousness we are not social.[10]

Dieter Brüll made an important distinction between asocial and antisocial. In his book on the Anthroposophical Social Impulse he wrote that we are asocial when we separate from others to develop ourselves. We are antisocial when we take earthly goods to consume them. Both asocial and antisocial belong to being human and are morally neutral. This changes when we impose the products of our spiritual development, our ideas on others, or exploit them so that we can consume more. Then law has to limit our asocial and antisocial possibilities to prevent a degradation of our fellow human beings into objects of indoctrination and exploitation. Rights (for the other) arise where we ask what is due to us in relation to our fellow human beings. A new social quality appears in society when law is thus created. As will be proposed later on, social threefolding is the path to allow social living.

Rudolf Steiner showed how a social impulse could become active in the human soul as the fruit of an inner development when the social element is brought into day consciousness from the world of night consciousness. This is connected to the awakening of our

---

10  Rudolf Steiner: *The Challenge of the Time*s (1918), Spring Valley 1941 (CW 186).

higher being (our individuality, also called the Self), itself a social process to a large degree, as will be described in the third chapter.

Steiner considered his Anthroposophical movement to be a preparation for a future culture of brotherhood and sisterhood that can develop in Eastern Europe and the rest of the world. This new social life, prepared in the undercurrents of modern culture, will then be able to unfold fully. Anthroposophy wants to help develop the necessary social forces. How Steiner imagined this to come about can be grasped by following the path on which he developed his ideas of renewing social life and by observing how he treated other people. These ideas form the developmental steps of the Anthroposophical Social Impulse, as Brüll called it.

## 2. The Social Impulse in Rudolf Steiner's Life

The social impulse marked a clear path in Rudolf Steiner's life. Dieter Brüll discovered a striking seven-year rhythm in which Steiner formulated his new vision of social life step by step. According to Brüll this rhythm started in 1884, when the 23-year-old Steiner published a small essay in a magazine in Hermannstadt (now in Romania) and ended 35 years later with the publication of the book, *Towards Social Renewal* in 1919.[11]

Steiner was still studying in Vienna in 1884, when he wrote in this essay "A Free Gaze into the Present" that it was the task of German culture to rethink in a spiritual sense what came from the West in science and politics. In this essay he made a remark that received a concrete form in social threefolding, namely: The state cannot

---

11  Rudolf Steiner: *Towards Social Renewal* (1919), London 1977 (CW 23).

free man, only education can do that, but the state has to see to it that everyone finds the soil on which his freedom can flourish.[12]

In 1891 Steiner traveled from Weimar, where he worked in the Goethe archives, to Vienna to give a lecture on Goethe's fairy tale of *The Green Snake and the Beautiful Lily*. Brüll supposed that in this lecture Steiner interpreted the motif of the four kings out of the social impulse. This fairy tale contains a poetic picture of social threefolding and emphasizes the joy of deep conversation.

These two steps were followed by the four foundational elements of the Anthroposophical Social Impulse. They are the Fundamental Sociological Law, the Fundamental Social Law, the Social Archetypal Phenomenon and social threefolding. They are only listed briefly here and will be elaborated on further in separate sections.

The Fundamental Sociological Law of 1898 describes the emancipation of modern society from social associations that curb individual development. Steiner's experiences with free thinkers, artists and anarchists from Berlin are the background to this law. These were the people standing outside of traditional associations and experiencing their freedom. They were people in search of a spiritual home.

Shortly after leaving the Workers' Education School in 1905 Steiner published his Fundamental Social Law. It deals with the principle of separating labor and income. It expressed his link with the world of workers and his intention to allow the idea of brotherhood, so important to Theosophists, to become concrete.

It was followed by a description of the archetypal phenomenon of communication, which is the basis of all social life. In 1918 Steiner stated it only once when he described what takes place in a conversation. But Brüll indicated that the origin of this theme could already be found in the lecture, held in 1912, *Love and its*

---

12  Rudolf Steiner: *Gesammelte Aufsätze zur Kultur- und Zeitgeschichte* (1887-1901), Dornach 1989 (CW 31).

*Meaning in the World*.[13] In the conscious exercise of this archetypal phenomenon of social life, love is activated between people. This can lead to a meeting in which Christ can be with them. This lecture on love has a special place in a series of important lecture cycles on Christ and provides the background to the theme of the archetypal phenomenon of human communication.

During the First World War, Rudolf Steiner saw the decline of Central Europe approaching ever closer. From 1917 on, the Russian Revolution and the political program of the American president Woodrow Wilson were particularly threatening. Steiner worked on two memoranda and presented the main outlines of the threefolding of the social organism to the public. Since it had little success he entered political action, and in 1919 published his book *Towards Social Renewal*. This was the sixth step.[14]

Dieter Brüll believed that the Anthroposophical Social Impulse was not yet completed when Rudolf Steiner died in 1925. He pointed to the year 1926 when the last, seventh step, might have been made by Steiner that could have led to the full establishment of the social impulse within the Anthroposophical movement. According to my understanding, there is still a next step. The social impulse is a path to community building that creates a sphere in which spiritual beings can inspire human communities. If in 1926 new communities had been created, then seven years later in 1933, the Anthroposophical movement would have been better prepared to meet Christ — whose Second Coming, according to Steiner (who would then have been 72 years old), would have begun.

---

13   Rudolf Steiner: *Erfahrungen des Übersinnlichen - Die Wege der Seele zu Christus* (1912), Dornach 1994 (CW 143).

14   Rudolf Steiner: *Towards Social Renewal* (1919), London 1977 (CW 23).

## 3. The Fundamental Sociological Law

At the end of the 19th century, scientific investigators of the social question tried to apply the principles of natural science — especially Darwinism — to the development of society. In 1898 Rudolf Steiner discussed a book by the German philosopher and sociologist Ludwig Stein in his articles "The Social Question" and "Freedom and Society". Steiner supported the search for laws of development specific to humanity's development. He expected the right consequences to be drawn courageously and radically from the available facts. According to Steiner, people like Stein lacked this courage, and compromised with the prevailing attitudes of the power of state.

In this review Steiner formulated a law of social development called the Fundamental Sociological Law, that implies radical consequences for the state's role in society. This fundamental law was already mentioned in the first chapter and should be quoted here in its entirety. Steiner wrote:

> In the early stages of cultural evolution mankind tends towards the formation of social units; initially the interests of individuals are sacrificed to the interests of those groupings; the further course of development leads to the emancipation of the individual from the interests of the groupings and to the unrestricted development of the needs and the capacities of the individual.[15]

From the perspective of this Fundamental Sociological Law, the power of social institutions over the individual has to decrease and finally cease. The state and other social structures must support and be of service to the free development of the individual as much as possible. The ideal of the state has to be the absence of rulership. Steiner represented a radical individualism carried by individual moral consciousness.

---

15  Rudolf Steiner: *Social Threefolding* (edited by Stephen E. Usher), Forest Row, 2018, p. 25.

This element of the Anthroposophical Social Impulse has important implications. The Fundamental Sociological Law places the individual path of development of the human being into a social frame that increasingly frees our unfolding needs and forces. We then have to set up social institutions in such a way that they become instruments and support for our development. Forces from the past that hinder individual development will be evoked if we neglect this law. They are unjustified forces at present and will lead to social catastrophes. The need for authority is one of them. Steiner perceived them in Marxism and the social democracy of his time, since both glorified state power. We see this now in technocracy (rule by experts and managers), subordinating people to rules and thus drastically opposing the Fundamental Sociological Law.

Building new social institutions and communities that can support free individual development is a future-oriented task that is still hard to imagine. Yet it is necessary to create free spheres where the individual is inspired to follow a developmental path within an increasingly powerful technocracy. Then spiritual life will be able to unfold based on the free association of individuals. We must begin immediately.

People who have freed themselves from the power of social institutions can then associate with others for support, or to care for people who cannot manage by themselves because their souls were harmed for some reason. This is the perspective of the Fundamental Sociological Law.

## 4. The Fundamental Social Law

The Fundamental Sociological Law speaks of the free unfolding of the needs and forces of the individual and is therefore of utmost importance to cultural development. On the other hand, the Fundamental Social Law (from 1905) relates to the economic cooperation of people. It is a very controversial law, interpreted in a variety of ways within the Anthroposophical movement.

The concern of the Fundamental Social Law is the relationship between labor and income that provides the basis of modern economy in which we sell our labor to receive income. Social democracy has accepted this principle as well, but Rudolf Steiner questioned that relationship. He did not ask for economic growth but the well-being of humanity, as we can read in the text of this law:

> The well-being of a total community of human beings working together becomes greater the less the individual demands the products of his achievement for himself. That is, the more of these products he passes on to his fellow workers and the more his own needs are not satisfied out of his own achievements, but out of the achievements of others.[16]

In 1905 and 1906, Steiner formulated this Fundamental Law of Social Life in three essays titled "The Science of the Spiritual and the Social Question" He intended to write a series of essays about how we can understand the fundamental forces of social life, similar to *How to Know Higher Worlds*.[17] The first essays did not find response among theosophists and he stopped. The often wealthy theosophists, living on rents and investment incomes, resisted considering the world of work. Many did not see that spiritual activity should go further than self-perfection.

In these essays Steiner emphasized that spiritual science is to contribute fruitfully to the fulfillment of the tasks posed by life, and that it should find its way into all practical areas of daily life. He wanted to make the true source of social life accessible through Anthroposophy. Steiner also emphasized that to solve social problems it is not enough to change prevailing social conditions. They

---
16  Ibid, p. 53.
17  Rudolf Steiner: *How to Know Higher Worlds* (1904-1905), Hudson 1994 (CW 10).

are brought about by people and express their thoughts and attitudes. We can see that all conditions in society are built on personal benefit; two centuries ago Adam Smith already formulated it as the basis of modern economy.

Steiner said that if we want to solve the social question out of a spiritual point of view, we have to start from the principle of non-egoistic, unselfish labor and reshape society for it to be truly possible. He suggested institutional structures where nobody can claim the fruits of his work for himself at any time. To the utmost possible degree these should be of service to the total community of human beings working together, and on the other hand we ourselves should be supported by the work of our fellow human beings. It is important to know that working for our fellow human beings and earning a certain income are two distinct issues. According to Steiner, only a person who works exclusively for others can gradually become a non-egotistical worker.

We cannot exert force over people to be of service to others in their work. We have to find a motif in the other human being in order to work for him. If we associate with a totality of people for the purpose of work, the totality needs to have a common ideal, a spiritual mission. Only a spiritual world view can bring about the spiritual ability in us and awaken the higher being that unites us with others. Here Steiner's thesis opens altogether new perspectives. We need not wait to realize the Fundamental Social Law in a distant future; individuals can work in the sense of this law and achieve healing progress in social life even now. Steiner said that certain communities have a special tendency to work in this direction, and other communities exist in whose disposition something is prepared. According to Steiner, everyone can work in the sense of this law in his own sphere. It is up to us as to how much well-being we realize.

On October 26, 1905, in the lecture *The Social Question and Theosophy,* Rudolf Steiner mentioned the possibility of forming income communities.[18] The participants collect their income in a joint bank account from which personal expenses are paid. This experiment was carried out at the GLS Bank in Germany, as well as in other Anthroposophical contexts.

The Anthroposophical movement has contributed very little, usually out of ignorance or under the assumption that this law is meant for a distant future. Many people have not yet noticed that employment relations are no longer appropriate to the times. Some think that the widespread division of labor, where people increasingly work for each other, confirms this law, or that the welfare state has already abolished the relationship of work and income to some degree. The latter is true, but it is strengthening egoism. Outside of Anthroposophy, we can observe Israeli kibbutzim, where people want to share their life and work with others out of a strong spiritual impulse. This original impulse, however, is very much weakened by lack of a spiritual world view.

In Anthroposophical circles the Fundamental Social Law came to life in the curative pedagogic institutions of Karl König's Camphill Movement. Often this is at the expense of the Fundamental Sociological Law for young co-workers insofar as their own development is left behind. Some therapeutic communities, Waldorf schools and economic initiatives share the common income in new, open communication. Factually, it is possible everywhere. But our society, suffused by the spirit of modern economics, makes it difficult to provide spiritually inspired initiatives with a different basis.

If Anthroposophy wants to prepare a new culture of brotherhood, the Fundamental Social Law must be taken seriously. Our work is still a commodity. We sell it to others in a spirit of selfishness. Here Steiner sees a leftover from the old condition of slavery. Work can become a sacrifice we bring with pleasure to someone in need of our service. The Fundamental Social Law helps us to develop so-

---
18   *Beiträge zur Rudolf Steiner Gesamtausgabe*, Nr. 88, Dornach 1988.

cial forms in which we can share the earth's products we receive as brothers and sisters. On this path we can learn to manage our antisocial drives.

On February 21, 1912, Rudolf Steiner gave yet another motif for realizing the Fundamental Social Law in work. He pointed out that a world order in which we have to earn what we need through work does not support a true fundamental conviction of reincarnation and karma.[19] The money I work for becomes a wall between others and myself and prevents my actions from being free and having a karmic effect.

## 5. The Archetypal Phenomenon of Social Life

In the beginning of this chapter it was mentioned that asocial and antisocial actions have an important place in our lives. They are related to drives that appear when we develop spiritually and consume something. At this level we are not yet colliding with others. Only when we force our ideas on others out of our asocial drive and exploit others out of our antisocial drive do we make the other into an object. Our drives must be curbed for the relationship to the other to be social. Then, out of a social impulse, we can make the need of the other the motif of our actions.

The effect of this social impulse relates to the previously elaborated laws. According to the Fundamental Sociological Law humanity frees itself from social institutions to develop its (asocial) inner life. Then, for example, as social beings we can help others in their development by forming communities that support individual development, or by simply listening without forcing an opinion. The Fundamental Social Law suggests the development of social structures in which we make our work available to others instead of exploiting them.

---
19   Rudolf Steiner: *Reincarnation and Karma* (1912), Hudson 1992 (CW 135).

In both situations the individual social impulse can be active only through concrete meetings where people can express their needs. The foundation of a new, conscious social life lies in encountering others, as, Rudolf Steiner often made clear. In a lecture held on December 12, 1918, in Bern he briefly describes what essentially occurs in each conversation we have with another. We have now arrived at the third element of the Anthroposophical Social Impulse. It is this fragment:

> When two people face each other, the one attempts to put to sleep the other and the other continuously tries to stay awake. This is, to speak in the Goethean sense, the archetypal phenomenon of social science.[20]

This lecture on social and unsocial drives relates to what Steiner said about the increased unsocial character of modern society and the necessity of giving instructions out of spiritual science to consciously order social life. He spoke of structures necessary to form inner social abilities, of the interest people can develop for each other, of pictures they can make of the other, and of meetings between people.

In this lecture Steiner said that we are social in our sleep and in waking we are social only when we are able to rescue something from sleep, by bringing it over into day-consciousness. He then described conversations between people as an unconscious process of sleeping into the other (listening) and awakening in oneself (speaking). If I want to understand what another person wants to say, I must be ready to be put to sleep (in a metaphorical sense) for as long as the other speaks. I give up my self-consciousness temporarily and to a certain extent, and due to this sacrifice the other can fill me with his or her being. In this condition I give myself entirely over to the other to perceive with full attention their individuality in what they say. In

---

20  Rudolf Steiner: *The Challenge of the Times* (1918), Spring Valley 1941 (CW 186).

this moment I am social, but only until my asocial drive cannot bear it any longer and I throw the other out of myself. Then I can say or ask something. Now it is a question of whether I can carry over into waking up what the other entrusted to me. To the degree to which I can hold this in my consciousness, I come to insights that I can bring into conversation by taking the word and putting the other to sleep.

It involves practicing two skills: freeing a space for the other so that he or she can speak undisturbed, and the ability to hold in awakening what the other said. In practice this proves very difficult, as many cannot listen and others cannot stop speaking. While listening, we can fall asleep so deeply that we forget everything upon awakening. Often the conversation does not take place from heart to heart but from head to head (where nobody falls asleep), or we speak to the emotions or the will of the other. There are also many situations in which we do not understand each other and a real meeting does not take place. The archetypal phenomenon of social life only leads to this encounter when we learn to manage it in consciousness. That is, when we can consciously follow the movement of the pendulum between falling asleep and awakening, and find the way to the heart of the other. We must develop abilities of soul like having a strong interest, listening, having presence of mind, objectivity, and the skill to understand the other from the inside. These abilities are much more difficult to manage in group conversation.

In conversation, of course, falling asleep and awakening do not take place in the common sense. They are two gestures. In falling asleep we find the female, sympathetic gesture and in awakening the male, the antipathetic gesture. Throughout this book female and male are not related to gender. In the sympathetic movement our soul opens to the other and tries to take the being of the other into our heart. Our forces of consciousness must be strengthened in order to understand what the other really wants to say. In falling asleep we pass over the threshold of the spiritual world and need an active, awake receptivity, as in meditation and real sleep, to live our spiritual experiences consciously. The gesture of awakening (when I can speak) means that in speaking I contact my higher being in another person. That is, in the space he or she creates inside for me. In group conversations a social space can only be created when we unite in respect and love.

The force of love lives in the archetypal phenomenon of social life. We always have to sacrifice self-consciousness to a certain extent to take the other into ourselves. The other person can then become the source of my social consciousness. We can, by giving back what we heard, unite the other more deeply with him or herself out of meeting his or her real being. Each question we ask can reveal something of the being, the inner life of the other person, and open altogether new perspectives for him or her. We can, as Dieter Brüll pointed out, think the thoughts of the other and experience them as complementing our truth. Then we carry a social element into the asocial life of spirit. An awareness of the other's need could be the motif of our actions and then we carry a social element into antisocial economic life. This makes it a deeply Christian social impulse. People who learn to consciously practice the archetypal phenomenon of communication through inner preparation and with morality can develop consciousness of Christ's presence in social life.

The great importance of good communication has been convincingly demonstrated by the American psychologist Marshall Rosenberg. In the method of non-violent communication he developed, he points out that in a conversation we often only listen in order to be able to react more sharply and be right. Good communication is listening in order to understand the other person better. If we have a conflict with each other, we can start by naming an actual observation. Then we can express our feelings without criticizing the other, and in a next step we can express our needs and finally make a request, in which the other must feel free to respond or not.

This archetypal phenomenon is of fundamental importance for the renewal of human life. We can hardly imagine how important it must be for people to truly meet each other, because then in listening attentively we create space for the other. In such conversations we can gain insight into our lives and the lives of others. Ideals can become conscious in conversation; they can be experienced and turned into impulses, and by experiencing them, impulses can be put into words and expressed in ideas. A consciousness of rights arises in meeting others when our sense of rights is spoken to. In meetings we can learn to understand others and make images of them. It can be therapeutic and healing, and can awaken the other through questions. Meeting others is also a path to meeting the Christ. In all these aspects, the archetypal phenomenon of social life has the same fundamental importance for the renewal of spiritual life. This will be described further in chapter three. The archetypal phenomenon of social life cannot yet activate social forces on the societal level; therefore, a threefold social structure is necessary.

## 6. Social Threefolding

In order to understand what Rudolf Steiner meant by social threefolding, we have to avoid a one-sided juristic approach. Threefolding does not only concern structures that create social forms and make laws and agreements, but also the social process that leads to them. Political life in society cannot be limited to laws and rules that order society. Everything of relevance to the creation of inter-human conditions must be addressed.

Relationships between people are increasingly problematic in modern society. An adequate political life can only arise when we stand next to each other as equals, without individual abilities and economic positions playing a role, and without using power. What is already difficult on a small scale becomes even more so on higher levels of social life, in particular with large groups of people. Economic or ideological interests, or a state apparatus's drive for rulership, increasingly dictate laws. The individual human being vanishes from the consciousness of the experts who control social processes and set rules for communal life. The possibility for individuals to order social life as equals is continuously decreasing in modern society.

Steiner's feelings on this were expressed in a statement he made in Dornach on January 31, 1920, when he said: "Either Bolshevism over the whole world, or threefolding! Maybe you don't like threefolding; then you opt for an old world order!"[21] Our future will be bolshevist (at that time the Communist rule in Russia. Today we would say a system under the control of technocrats or managers), unless we realize social threefolding. One year later, on January 2, 1921, Steiner said: "It is impossible to build Central and Eastern Europe on a foundation other than threefolding."[22] These words have not lost their validity after the disintegration of Communism and the rise of bureaucracy in the European Union.

With social threefolding Steiner wanted to create conditions that would allow humanity to live socially; that is, to develop social relationships with others. He did not proceed from the ideal human being, but from common people with their asocial and antisocial drives. Threefolding is a frame within which we can develop our social drives. Steiner said that an instinctive threefolding existed until the Middle Ages, but with the rise of a world economy the time when social structures could be built out of instincts has passed. It is of utmost importance now to consciously create threefolding. It

---

21  Rudolf Steiner: *What is Necessary in these Urgent Times?* (1920), Forest Row 2010 (CW 196).

22  Rudolf Steiner: *Communicating Anthroposophy* (1921), Great Barrington 2015 (CW 338).

lives as a goal in our unconscious, and everyone–no matter where he or she is–has the social task to work on it. In schools we must develop a feeling of how the forces of the social organism should work in a healthy way. Every era demands different social forms, and threefolding does not have an eternal character, either. Steiner said on September 28, 1919:

> Threefolding has now become necessary through the demand of the time, and a time will come again when threefolding must be overcome. But that is not today, that is the time of three to four hundred years from now.[23]

Steiner developed the basic outlines of a threefold social organism in two memoranda in 1917.[24] He spoke of dismantling the unitary state and creating three autonomous sub-systems: spiritual life (culture), political life, and economic life. Based on their interests in the sphere of culture, people will associate in corporations that can establish their own courts, schools, churches, etc. Everyone can freely join these functional, professional and national corporations. A representation of people will look after the purely political, military and policing affairs in political life. And an economic parliament will order the affairs of economic life, supported by associations of objective cooperation that can arise there. The state should limit itself to protecting law and order.

Steiner went even further with this concept. He explained that spiritual life is concerned with the unfolding abilities of individuals, political life with the relationship from one to the other (to be regulated by law), and economic life with the relationship of the individual to the outer world. The latter is formed in production, circulation and consumption of goods (and services), and can be

---

23  Rudolf Steiner: *Geisteswissenschaftliche Behandlung sozialer und pädagogischer Fragen* (1919), Dornach 1991 (CW 192).

24  Rudolf Steiner: "Memoranda of 1917", in: *Rudolf Steiner, Social Threefolding* (edited by Stephen E. Usher), Forest Row, 2018.

organized in associations where representatives of these three spheres of economic life can observe the economic process and make appropriate decisions on prices, levels of production, quality, etc.

Again, in his book *Towards Social Renewal* (1919), Rudolf Steiner concretized his ideas in relation to the actual condition in Southwest Germany, sketching possible applications for that situation. He made these suggestions based on Anthroposophy, but emphasized that threefolding is about forms that can be ordered differently out of various views and social impulses. Social threefolding is not a model but a way of thinking to find solutions for practical problems in accordance with its basic principles.

On the basis of Anthroposophy, Steiner indicated that humanity can realize the impulse of freedom. Freedom to develop individual skills and freedom for the other to be protected from my asocial drives in spiritual life. In political life humanity can strive to realize the idea of equality, and in economic life the cooperation of people can be based on brotherhood, with our antisocial drives curbed by associations. The three ideals of the French Revolution: freedom, equality and brotherhood, would then find their place in social life.

Steiner wanted to intervene in the state of affairs of the time by proposing the idea of social threefolding. Germany had been dragged into a war that took a critical turn in 1917 and Central European culture was exposed to social chaos (The First World War, 1914-1918). It was a matter of life or death for the German nation and its spiritual task within European culture, Steiner said. The German Empire, established in 1871, lacked any spiritual ideal, and had fallen victim to Prussian militarism. The catastrophic war threatened Central Europe to be run over by ideas from the West, and Steiner presented social threefolding in this context as a social impulse belonging to the essence of the Central European cultural task. But from 1917 on this task was also threatened by the opposing impulse of Bolshevism.

Between 1917 and 1922 Rudolf Steiner continued to point to this social mission of Central Europe out of new situations and opportunities for action. Central Europe was for him the cultural area that was politically organized by both the German and the Austro-Hungarian Empires, and those areas that were strongly influenced by German culture. Not only Germany, but also Austria and Switzerland belonged to it, along with the Baltic States, Poland, the Czech Republic, Slovakia, Hungary, Slovenia and Croatia. Central Europe is the area that was politically splintered and culturally destroyed by the two world wars.

The 1917 peace program of the American president Woodrow Wilson, proposing the new formation of Central and Eastern Europe on the basis of Western ideas and interests, received Steiner's full attention. Its central idea was the right of self-determination of nations and, more concretely, the idea of certain Central European nations to establish their own state. When members of various nations live together without clear-cut boundaries (this was and is still the case in Central Europe), the formation of nation-states could only lead to chaos, for each new state had to reckon with the problem of minorities.

Steiner's memoranda for politicians in Germany and Austro-Hungary presented the idea of cultural autonomy for Central European nations and a federated association for the nations living in Austro-Hungary. His starting point was not the right of self-determination of nations but the right of self-determination of free individuals. He also summoned Germany to discuss clearly the causes of the war with regards to the question of war debts, later to be of great importance, and to resist Wilson's attempt to make Central Europe dependent on Anglo-Saxon world rule. If Central Europe would not come up with its own peace program, it would, according to Steiner, end up in a state of economic slavery. Through influential Anthroposophists Steiner tried to motivate the German and Austrian leadership to pronounce social threefolding as their own Central European program of peace, instead of Wilson's program. However, leading politicians lacked the necessary courage.

The German Empire experienced a military breakdown in 1918 that led to the proclamation of the Republic in November of that same year. Following the Russian example, councils of workers and soldiers took power in dozens of cities. Anthroposophists like Emil Molt, Carl Unger and Hans Kuhn from Stuttgart searched for ways to contribute to economic reforms. Rudolf Steiner advised them to found free schools to separate the cultural life from the state. He wanted to activate the German nation spiritually. On March 5, 1919, he published a proclamation: An die Deutsche Nation und die Kulturwelt [To the German Nation and the Cultural World], in which he called for the dissolution of the unitary state and the implementation of social threefolding. This proclamation was soon signed by many, including prominent non-Anthroposophists from liberal circles. On April 22, 1919, they met in Stuttgart and founded the Association for threefolding the social organism.

Rudolf Steiner held conferences and tried to awaken an understanding of threefolding in Anthroposophical circles. *Towards Social Renewal*, published at the end of April 1919, originated from these conferences. April of that same year saw upheavals among workers in many cities. A council republic was proclaimed in Munich and strikes took place everywhere. Steiner opened his book by asking what proletarians really wanted and concluded that they were looking for a spiritual life in which their human dignity was acknowledged, and an economic life where labor was not a commodity. Out of these viewpoints he systematically developed his idea of social threefolding, with labor as a problem to be solved in the political and not the economic life.

The proletariats seemed to be open to the ideas of threefolding. From the end of April onwards Steiner held numerous lectures for workers in large factories in and around Stuttgart, which showed his great familiarity with their problems. These lectures were received well by the workers. More than 12,000 people from liberal and social democratic circles signed a resolution for Steiner to be appointed by the government of Wurttemberg (the southwestern part of Germany) to inaugurate threefolding. This was not his initiative. The social democratic government and leading industrialists were dismissive. Steiner did not find a connection to them, but to the left socialist workers' committees.

An action for a radical system of workers' councils was initiated, going much further than the law on a workers' council prepared by the government. Steiner saw a starting point for an associative economy in the workers' councils, and he stood behind the radical workers. He spoke on behalf of workers' councils, with engineers and managers to be voted in as well, and for bringing the workers' councils of Wurttemberg into an economic parliament. Steiner wanted to win over the bourgeoisie as well, but the bourgeois public addressed by Steiner was reluctant and, as the prominent socialist Siegfried Dorfner pointed out, did not believe that threefolding could be the foundation on which the bourgeoisie and the proletariat would be able to come to a mutual understanding. The entrepreneurs did not accept limitations to power, nor did the left parties and unions want to support a council system they could not control. Too few active Anthroposophists joined Steiner's threefolding actions, and the movement for autonomous workers' councils failed.[25]

In June 1919 Steiner tried to initiate a council movement for cultural life. He called for a culture council to place education outside of the state. Non-Anthroposophists such as the German writer Thomas Mann, for example, signed this appeal, but the bourgeoisie did not want to associate with it. The first free school, the Stuttgart Waldorf School, arose out of this initiative because the workers at

---

25   Rudolf Steiner: *Betriebsräte und Sozialisierung* (1919), Dornach 1989 (CW 331).

the cigarette factory Waldorf Astoria requested a school for their children.

A new threefolding initiative began in 1920 with the stock company Der Kommende Tag [The Approaching Day]. It wanted to create a financial basis for Anthroposophical work and connect the various Anthroposophical businesses with each other. Steiner hoped that a model for other businesses would arise, but he soon noticed the lack of people with economic and social skills. The stock company was financially ruined, but laid the foundation for important initiatives such as scientific research and the production of medicinal remedies (Weleda).

Immediately after the First World War opportunities for social alternatives still existed, and Steiner and his co-workers used this space as far as possible. Several years later the social fronts hardened and possibilities for threefolding to accomplish something on the societal level vanished. Steiner concluded in 1922 that the time for large actions had passed and the movement for threefolding had failed. Some Anthroposophists concluded that threefolding was not important to Anthroposophy anymore, or even that Steiner erred. For others, threefolding was the last station of a long prepared development and a future orientation.

In *Towards Social Renewal,* Rudolf Steiner indicated that he had developed his knowledge of the social organism based on a comparison of the functioning of the human organism with the functioning of social life. After more than thirty years of research Steiner arrived at three subsystems, each with their own functions within the whole of the human organism. They are the nerve-sense system, the rhythmical system of breathing and circulation, and the metabolic-limb system. These systems interweave. Outside the metabolic system, for example, metabolic activities take place in the other two subsystems as well. The idea of threefolding the social organism came out of this perception of the human being.

Steiner made clear that the healthy relationship of the three social sub-systems was disturbed in modern society. The unitary state developed and dismantled the membering of the social organism or did not accommodate it. Thus the state controlled an important part of spiritual life, and education in particular. Economic life encroached upon political life and dictated public jurisdiction. These violations of boundaries have grown since Steiner's time, and economic life vehemently encroached into spiritual life as well. The consequence was that education became adjusted to the demands of economy and the human spirit became human capital. Economy turned everything into commodity, even labor rights and the human spirit, which should never be sold.

Steiner criticized the existing labor, capital and land market. These were not comparable to commodities that could be bought and consumed. In the past labor was slave labor, and modern wage labor is a remnant of this system. Instead of his labor the free person can only sell the products of his labor. Capital is a destructive force when it seeks to grow without limits. Originally, money was a legal document. A farmer who stored his grain in an Egyptian temple received a shard on which the year and the quantity was written. For this shard the farmer received grain in a following year when he needed it, but less than he had deposited. These shards developed into means of exchange, and later became money. Land is not produced by people. It is a gift of nature that is held in collective property in ancient societies. For the economy it is not crucial who owns the land, but who has the right to use it. The same is the case for companies.

This also means that the shareholders of a company should not influence the management of the company. In order to guarantee the corporate social responsibility of companies, the shares can be placed in a foundation. This is called "steward ownership." Such forms of enterprise already exist in the Netherlands, Germany, Denmark and other countries. Based upon social threefolding, Armin Steuernagel and Gerald Häfner, among others, have worked out a legal form for this in Germany.

To Rudolf Steiner, the question of labor was a legal question to be solved in political life. Capital should be made available to skilled businessmen by institutions of spiritual life in the form of a right to use. Agricultural land and other means of production such as enterprises should be administered by the community and provided for use only for a limited time.

Threefolding society must in particular focus on the sphere of political life in which people make decisions together, since it is by now nearly entirely undermined in Western societies and will be altogether abolished by technocrats and managers if it does not encounter resistance. It will be crucial to rebuild political life within the polarity of spiritual and economic life. Threefolding should find a starting-point from the center of social life; i.e., political life, where the whole society can be ordered. Here we find its nucleus: the social organism must have a heart, a place where every human being can find him or herself principally in full equality to others, where justice can arise out of a consciousness of rights. This consciousness lives as a strong impulse in the democratization movement since the late 1960s.

Rudolf Steiner did not indicate concretely how this political sphere, the sphere of rights and duties, could be set up. Today we have parliaments, and Steiner was not a great friend of English parliamentarism. In his memoranda of 1917 he spoke against accepting this system in Central Europe, since it would be a tool for economic interest groups. It would deliver Central Europe to Anglo-American world rule. For a consciousness of rights to function properly, we need institutions that express the political consciousness of the citizenship.

We may think of forms of direct democracy like referendums (as they exist in Switzerland and other countries) and citizens' forums that arose in 1989 in Eastern Germany and Czechoslovakia. These countries showed how political parties encroached upon the citizens' forums to monopolize opinions or decisions for different interest groups. Here lies a clear task of social threefolding: to develop new forms of political life. In recent years, in many countries and at many levels, people have been asked to take a one-off seat in European citizens' assemblies that are representative of the population in terms of composition. They are given access to the necessary information and enter into dialogue with each other in order to jointly formulate advice for new legislation.

Threefolding does not end on the level of society (macro level). Usually Anthroposophical circles consider social threefolding not applicable to the meso level. But we can also find the three spheres within institutions of spiritual and economic life (the meso level), but they don't have the same autonomy as on the macro level. Each school, as an institution of spiritual life, can have, next to the essential spiritual organ (the circle of teachers), a no less important but usually non-existent, economic organ in which the need for education is brought forth. Between them a sphere of rights can be created that forms its heart. Here decisions can be made and mandates given. Only those people who carry the consequences should belong in this central body and make these decisions.

The economic sphere is essential to the institutions of economic life; i.e., production-oriented businesses, but also we should find there a spiritual sphere where human abilities are developed and a sphere of rights where decisions are made.

Rudolf Steiner did not directly speak of organizing institutions in this meso sphere in the sense of social threefolding, but he indicated indirectly that we could start with threefolding right away, as with the congregations of the Christian Community. In his book *Waldorf*

*School and the Threefold Structure*, Dieter Brüll sketched the basic form of a threefold school as a practical example.[26] He mentioned that the Waldorf School was born out of the threefold movement and that Steiner considered it to be the germ of the future rebirth of social threefolding.

But we see in practice that the central sphere of rights is hardly developed in most Anthroposophical institutions. The group representing the spiritual or economic side, or even a fourth group or body, the executive, makes decisions. The law often demands an executive who represents the institution to the outside world. However, this executive can give its internal power to the body of rights. Many Anthroposophical institutions have a director who is not connected to Anthroposophy and runs the institution as a manager without a sphere of rights.

Workers' councils, common in Europe today, do not represent the function of this central body, either. This means that many people, connected existentially to the organization or institution and dependent on it for their existence, are actually not able to take part in decisions within the organization. We may say, with Steiner, that the disappearance of the sphere of rights is Bolshevism (rule by experts). The individual human being within the institution becomes an object of ambition and intolerance (in the sphere of spiritual life), greed (in the sphere of economic life) and the thirst for power (in pseudo-political life).

From another point of view we can say that we have not yet learned to build a true political life, nor discovered that we can avoid these negative qualities with social threefolding. We can curb these qualities in social life through structural means, not by educating people. Threefolding is necessary until we have overcome these asocial and antisocial characteristics from the inside out. We can realize

---

26  Dieter Brüll: *The Waldorf School and the Threefold Structure*, Fair Oaks 2003.

it only once we have given up our claims for power over others. A sphere of rights arises only to the degree that we relinquish power.

Why did the Anthroposophical movement not take up the impulse of social threefolding? The most important reason seems to be that too little consciousness of rights exists in the Anthroposophical movement. People are fully occupied with their work and leave decisions to spiritual authorities or financial experts. A hollowed-out consciousness of rights combined with a general bourgeois spirit that neutralizes all radical movements has become the norm in our society.

Old Roman ideas of law with authoritarian and hierarchical structures in which personalities from spiritual or economic life reign, continue to live in the bourgeoisie. The former consciousness of freedom in Germanic law, with its important role in the Middle Ages and in the transition into modern times (such as the free cities and the peasants' and citizens' fights for freedom), has vanished. Political life is imprisoned in old structures and has to re-awaken.

It has already been indicated that the sphere of rights embraces all human relationships. It is the sphere of social interaction, the purely human sphere, with a juristic aspect as part of it. In this (political) sphere we order our society, our organizations and our groups. By making agreements and rules, creating laws, social forms and structures we constitute this sphere of rights.

On the meso level, organizations and groups in particular provide possibilities for the development of social consciousness, but we must still learn to realize them. On the macro level the Anthroposophical movement has also learned to live with a consciousness of rights that has been corrupted by technocracy instead of trying to heal society through social threefolding. Representatives of the movement preferred to achieve special positions through personal contact with well-meaning officials. Instead of fighting for educational freedom for all educational streams, the Waldorf movement acquired special privileges in some European countries. Well-meaning officials have now been substituted by functionaries who no longer grant exemptions, but want to create uniformity in all states belonging to the European Union.

Fortunately, since 1990 an active European Forum for Freedom in Education exists that connects people from more than 30 countries, and in which Anthroposophists play a leading role. For more than ten years there has also been ELIANT (the European Alliance of Initiatives of Applied Anthroposophy) in which these initiatives work together and represent their interests at the international level.

Not only education but also curative pedagogy, health care, and farming, etc. experienced this process of state regulation in Europe. Any renewal in these areas, whether realized by Anthroposophy or other spiritual movements, runs the risk of being destroyed in a new societal reality unless we are willing to leave the domain controlled by the state and build organizations and communities out of our own strength. This seems to be the price for what was neglected in the sixties; namely, to fight for a basic income and a school voucher, in addition to children's allowance in order to finance the school of one's choice), education money for students (to finance one's own education), and freedom of therapy, insurance, etc. These are issues of the sphere of rights and concrete applications of social threefolding. Free and mature people who work in these areas should decide on questions of education and health, not officials.

The reason for a barely developed consciousness of rights in the Anthroposophical movement is a poor understanding of the social impulse. The threefolding impulse was a reality for Rudolf Steiner. In his conscious impulses there lived archetypal thoughts concerning social life, while they lived more or less unconsciously in the instinctive life of their contemporaries. By activating the threefolding impulse in society, Steiner wanted to give modern humanity the opportunity to think the thoughts of the other in spiritual life, to experience equality in relation to the other in the practice of political life, and to work out of the other's needs in economic life. These are, as Dieter Brüll remarked, three aspects of the social impulse of Anthroposophy immediately connected to the activity of Christ within. Thus the work of social threefolding appears as a path of humanizing social life, a path to liberate humanity and increase social well-being, and a path to practical Christianity.

The other human beings who increasingly disappeared from vision because they had become an object in modern society appear again in consciousness through social threefolding on the macro and meso level. On the micro level they appear as living reality through a conscious exercise of the archetypal phenomenon of communication where one must inwardly make room for them. Our consciousness must make a sacrifice, and we don't like that. Nor does it fit well with a path on which Anthroposophy is merely understood as a means to develop consciousness, where only spiritual life is considered to be real and social life irrelevant. It is good to mirror ourselves in Rudolf Steiner to overcome this inner attitude.

## 7. Rudolf Steiner as Social Person

The failed action of social threefolding was a great personal disappointment to Rudolf Steiner. His untiring application to this cause shows his willingness to do what the situation of the time demanded, however uncertain the course of events might be. Later, he said about threefolding: "I knew that people were not yet mature, but it had to be tried. I could have erred."

This application to the needs of the time and the concern for the needs of people coming to him even when he knew that they would often disappoint him, distinguishes Steiner. A large number of his students described this social attitude in memoirs. The Russian author

Andrej Belyi, who experienced him closely for four years and called him the "unexpected joy" of his life, wrote most impressively. But he, too, described in his book *Verwandeln des Lebens* [Transforming Life] only a few facets of Rudolf Steiner, the human being.[27] When we deeply engage in descriptions of Steiner we arrive at a picture of a completely free, unconventional and non-bourgeois person with well-integrated male and female aspects of soul who, in cooperation with women like Marie von Sivers, the English sculptor Edith Maryon and Ita Wegman, achieved great creative accomplishments.

Steiner was an utterly modest person, reserved and never forcing his opinion on others. He never judged people, but only, when necessary, their actions or attitudes. He is described as a sociable and humorous person, enjoying the company of others. Belyi pointed to his unlimited love and compassion, and the patience he had with others. Few people know about Steiner's connection to his parents and concern for his brother and sister.

Steiner understood himself as a teacher of freedom. He left people free when they had to make decisions. He wanted only to advise. He never interfered with the freedom of another, even when important issues were at hand. He held back his personal intentions and interests, his sympathies and antipathies, to bring others to experiencing freedom and realizing their spiritual possibilities. He once wrote in a letter that he wanted to bring his students to a path of development. Steiner applied what he wrote in the first chapter of *How to Know Higher Worlds*:

> No teacher of spiritual life exercises dominion over other human beings by means of such rules. Such teachers do not seek to restrict anyone's autonomy.[28]

---

27  Andrej Belyi: *Verwandeln des Lebens*, Basel 1975.
28  Rudolf Steiner: *How to Know Higher Worlds* (1904-1905), Hudson 1994 (CW 10).

In the prologue to *Cosmic Memory,* Steiner rejected any claim to infallibility.[29] The initiate can err as well and usually cannot perceive or describe all aspects of an issue. Again and again he appealed to "healthy common sense" and our "natural sense of truth". We should not accept anything on the initiate's authority, but learn to trust our inner wisdom. We can learn that only our own experiences can be the starting point in spiritual affairs.

Steiner continuously made himself available to others. He enjoyed questions that were brought to him and freed himself entirely to help people. Belyi says that he received wings with Steiner's help. Friedrich Rittelmeyer described how when Steiner took leave of him, he thanked him for the opportunity he had provided to help him. People noticed in Steiner's lectures how he perceived their life situations and gave the answers they needed. In personal conversations this took place in a concentrated form. Steiner inwardly made room for the other, fell asleep into them while the other came to him or herself and felt altogether understood and confirmed by Steiner.

The Scottish anthroposophist Daniel Nicol Dunlop remarked in 1935 that Rudolf Steiner seemed to give his whole nature to understanding another person, that he looked for possibilities, not failures, and thus inspired the highest in people. According to Dunlop, Steiner met people so that those who recognized him could become human beings in the fullest sense of the word. Many described being inwardly awakened by Steiner. They received a new connection to themselves and suddenly saw clearly what they had to do with their life. Belyi described how the "hidden ground of his will" opened in the first meeting with Steiner. A picture of the "countenance of his soul" appeared and Rudolf Steiner was the mirror of his own higher being.

These experiences make clear that meetings between people can open unknown dimensions. Some had these experiences through

---

29　Rudolf Steiner: *Cosmic Memory* (1904-1908), New York 1990 (CW 11).

Steiner, but these experiences are possible in any real meeting. The intention of this brief eulogy is not to describe Steiner as an extraordinary human being, but as an example for anyone who wants to develop his social impulse. Steiner's humanness shows the credibility of his social impulse and stimulates us to develop relationships with others on our path of inner development, as he did.

The social impulse leads me to inwardly make room for others so that they can speak about their needs and I can freely and consciously relate to these needs out of my own possibilities. It demands a certain development of soul, but Steiner also showed how Anthroposophy could create a space in social life where people can become visible in their needs as human beings. The image of the other can reappear in our social consciousness. The social impulse can accomplish this in society as well. I will elaborate the meaning of an image of the other in the next chapter.

Dieter Brüll described the social impulse in his book as the Christ impulse of our time. The social impulse lives outside of Anthroposophy as well, because it ignites directly in a meeting insofar as Christ can be among the people who meet each other. Not one Anthroposophical initiative will be able to survive without the social impulse, because it is the heart of Anthroposophy. The same is true for all other spiritually based initiatives. More generally, without this social impulse social life will become more and more inhuman.

With the social impulse Anthroposophy received a path of development of our heart forces. We know Anthroposophy usually as a path of development of consciousness where thinking and willing interweave. But in the social impulse we have to sacrifice self-consciousness ever again to take the other into ourselves. It takes place in the core of our being, in our heart. The particular path of development of the heart forces is not the male path of cognition but the female path of empathy, sensibility and social feeling, always oriented to the other human being, increasingly reaching purity. Compassion and interest in the other then deepen into the force of love.

This social path brings us to a future culture of brotherhood in which man takes the other into his inner being, as Steiner described. Here we see something of a future socially focused Manichean Christianity (founded by the 3rd century Iranian prophet Mani) that seeks to overcome evil through gentleness. We saw how the Fundamental Sociological Law can lead to communities that help the individual, while the Fundamental Social Law can move us to consider our labor as a sacrifice or a gift we offer to someone else. This idea of offering labor as a gift to others has also been developed by the American author Charles Eisenstein in his book *Sacred Economics*. The impulse of creating social forms for the future is also connected to Manichaeism. On November 11, 1904, Steiner stated that Manicheans have the task of creating social forms in which true Christian life can take place.[30] Social threefolding is one of its expressions.

In order to bring the social impulse to development we must do inner work. We cannot be social out of our ego, but only out of our higher being. As long as we are not yet social we may create, through social threefolding, conditions for social behavior that allow our asocial and antisocial drives to exist only where they cannot be harmful. This does not make us into social beings. Social forms can certainly help us become social. After all, to come to self-consciousness and awaken spiritually is also a social process in which we can mutually support each other.

This awakening will be described in the next chapter. It is about the new possibilities that have arisen to develop a higher consciousness in conversations with each other and to gain insights that were previously only given to initiates, in the cooperation with each other.

---

30  Rudolf Steiner: *The Temple Legend* (1904-1914), London 1985 (CW 93).

CHAPTER III

# FROM OLD TO NEW MYSTERIES

## 1. A Revolution in Spiritual Life

When Rudolf Steiner became General Secretary of the German section of the Theosophical Society in 1902, he spoke about practical karma exercises in his first lecture. He wanted to help his listeners to perceive their own destiny by treating the karma of historical personalities. Karma is not an accidental burden but something we create ourselves. In karma we are dealing with the consequences of our actions from the past (old karma), but also with actions in the present that have consequences in the future (new karma). It is our destiny that forms, takes its course and changes in concrete relationships with others. Steiner wanted to help his listeners fathom their own destiny. This fundamental intention was rejected by the Theosophists and he had to wait until the time was ripe in 1924.

Understanding and ordering the positive and negative old karma we share with others provides a possibility for common work on a new culture. Ordering karma was for Steiner a condition for the work he wanted to start in 1923 at the Christmas Conference. The people around him had come from different historical streams that in some cases had been enemies, such as church people and heretics. This negative karma between them had to be understood and transformed so that Anthroposophists from different streams could find a way to work together for a common goal. Working together also requires that we learn to solve conflicts, heal social relations and forgive others for their mistakes.

Steiner wanted to gather a group of people and accompany them in their development to lay the foundation for a new spiritual culture based on inspiration from the time spirit Michael. He indicated that, according to spiritual tradition, the Archangel Michael is the time spirit for 354 years, from 1879 onward. Michael helps to reshape our thinking into an instrument with which we can enter the world of spirit. He counts on our courage and enthusiasm to fight materialism. He counts on people to act out of inner morality and ignite within themselves the inner sun of the Christ impulse. Michael's inspirations are strengthened because an era of five thousand years of spiritual darkness, the so-called Kali Yuga, which began in 3101 BC, expired in 1899, and spiritual light can stream to earth again, coinciding with the beginnings of Anthroposophy.

Steiner had to hold back his intentions while teaching in the Theosophical Society. Its members searched for their own spiritual experiences and Steiner helped them as teacher with personal instructions and great devotion. Only a few had the need to unite their spiritual development to everyday life and make it fruitful there. From the Christmas Conference of 1923 on this was to be different.

People were to build a new culture with the fruits of their spiritual development in cooperation with each other. Therefore, this conference is the beginning of a new mystery culture, a new spiritually inspired culture. We can describe "mysteries" as forms of communication with spiritual beings, which used to be possible in all cultures and changed over time as a result of changes in human consciousness. In certain cultures, consciousness expanding means are still used to experience these beings.

Previous to the Kali Yuga era, the mystery temples were the true centers of culture, where people walked an inner path that led to initiation (an opening of the organs of spiritual perception). Religion, art and science formed a whole and were cultivated by priests who, due to their initiation, had a connection to the world of divine forces. The mysteries represented the severely protected knowledge concerning the connection with spiritual beings that was the foundation of these cultures. Examples of such mystery centers were the temple complexes of Heliopolis and Karnak in Egypt, Eleusis and Samothrace in Greece, Ephesus in Asia Minor and the Externsteine in Germany.

The priests and the priest kings of ancient cultures were educated in such mystery centers to take care of the connection with the divine powers and to be inspired by them. A long preparation, during which they had to purify their souls and pass through several tests, preceded their initiation. This initiation was a procedure that lasted for 3 ½ days and took place in a condition of deep sleep, during which their organs of spiritual perception (chakras) were opened and their soul made a journey through the spiritual world.

Beginning with the Kali Yuga era these connections were gradually lost, until they had vanished almost everywhere in the centuries before Christ's birth. In Europe we find the last mystery schools in Ireland. Celtic missionaries brought these Hybernian Mysteries to mainland Europe, where they connected with the Grail Mysteries and functioned until the 9th century. In the age of Michael, we can unite religion, art, and science again in a new spiritual culture, where we can once more find entrance to the spiritual world, but now on the basis of a new self-conscious relationship with the world of spirit. This can take place in new mysteries. The Dutch Christian Community priest Bastiaan Baan has written an insightful book about these old and new mysteries.[31]

According to Rudolf Steiner, Christ created the possibility of these new conscious initiations. They can be called self-initiations and usually take place in four phases:

1. The cleansing and transformation of the soul to activate the chakras in the astral body.
2. The enlightenment, in which these organs of perception imprint themselves in the etheric body. The spiritual world then appears in images in our imaginative consciousness.
3. Entering into the world of the harmony of the planetary spheres. The work on the etheric body ensures that we develop an inspirational consciousness in which we hear the spiritual world speak.
4. Entering the world of spiritual beings. In our intuitive consciousness we can then perceive these beings.

Whereas each went an individual path in the old mysteries, in which the initiations took place in an unconscious condition, modern initiations require our awakened I-consciousness. In our time an initiation can lead to a conscious communication and cooperation with spiritual beings. This has been prepared for in ancient Israel, in the tradition of the Holy Grail, by the Cathars, the Knights Templar and the Brotherhood of the Rosicrucians in the late middle Ages. In the new mysteries it will no longer be about the transmission of

---

[31] Bastiaan Baan: *Old and New Mysteries,* Edinburgh 2014.

wisdom from the spiritual world, but about the use of the will, about the power of initiative of individuals who connect with each other.

The new mysteries have an individual and a social aspect. People who have developed a higher consciousness, such as Rudolf Steiner among others, can communicate in a conscious way as individuals, each on their own level, with spiritual beings. In addition, it is possible to work together in a group in such a way that the consciousness increases and the members of the group can receive inspirations from these beings. This is a way for the future, which is being developed in research groups. In small groups people have already gained experience with this.

Steiner wanted to create a modern mystery school in the School for Spiritual Science in Dornach. He inaugurated new mysteries in which the principle of initiation should once more become an effective force in all areas of human life. The path to initiation which he described in his book *How to Know Higher Worlds* retains its basic significance as an individual path. Many people have developed clairvoyant faculties in a natural way or by doing exercises, but it is only after an initiation that one can do spiritual research and cooperate with spiritual beings in a personal way, as Steiner did. We can then consciously pass the threshold of the spiritual world.

The conscious connection with the spiritual world received very important social aspects. Steiner could not alone create a new culture. For this he needed communities of co-workers on their path to their initiation. Together they can, in my understanding, consciously build a "social etheric" temple in their common work, in which they can be inspired by spiritual beings. It is a temple that can arise in a group in the etheric space. After all, the forces with which we connect socially and form communities lie in the etheric. On September 12, 1910, Steiner said: "The power to connect with other people lies in the etheric body."[32]

---

32   Rudolf Steiner, *The Gospel of Matthew*, Great Barrington 2002 (CW 123).

In all our social groups we usually unconsciously create an etheric field and an astral field in which so-called "doubles" are active. These are beings that we ourselves have formed in our physical, etheric and astral bodies in previous lives. They feed on the negative substance of actions, habits, emotions, feelings and thoughts that we do not control with our consciousness. In order to constantly receive new nourishment, they can start to steer our behaviour from our subconscious, as can be observed in an alcoholic or in someone who gets angry all the time because of trivial things. It is only by consciously controlling our behaviour that these doubles are transformed. C.G. Jung described them psychologically as "shadows." In groups, individual doubles can connect with each other to become group doubles.

By dealing with each other in a conscious manner and working together in a positive way a group creates an energetic field, an etheric structure in which spiritual beings (including the deceased ones) can descend, and if the group is open to this, can be inspiring. Groups that have existed for some time attract group angels and other inspirational beings. In fact, groups and organizations always attract beings. In the Anthroposophical world there is often little awareness of this. The etheric structure that people build up in their groups can become a temple or a place for demons. It depends on the intentions of the people what kind of beings manifest in it.

The image of the building of a temple played a central role in Steiner's Esoteric School (1904-1914), where he spoke in May 1905 about the meaning of *The Temple Legend* in relation to the building of the Solomonic Temple. This was exactly one lunar node (18 years and 7 month) before the Christmas Conference of 1923. According to Steiner, in meditation one builds a "hut" in the spiritual world. In the work of the Esoteric School he used the image of a spiritual temple. Its connection with the "social etheric" temple will be explained later.

We find the first steps towards these new I-conscious mysteries not only in Anthroposophy, but also in the School of the White Brotherhood of the Bulgarian spiritual teacher Peter Deunov (1864-1944), who can be considered a spiritual brother of Rudolf Steiner, and in the Stoa School of the Cypriote spiritual teacher and healer Daskalos (1912-1995). Also in movements not belonging to esoteric Christianity this new way of working together with spiritual beings is possible. What kind of beings they are depends on the moral quality of these movements.

The spiritual revolution that Steiner carried out comprised both the revelation of knowledge that was kept secret in the past and the public presentation of the new individual path of initiation for a conscious dealing with spiritual beings. It also included a social path to the spiritual renewal of culture that proceeds from these new mysteries.

The new mystery school Rudolf Steiner wanted to found brings us into cooperation with others in social life. It brings a social principle into spiritual life, whereas the social impulse of Anthroposophy brings spiritual principles into social life. Steiner inaugurated the new mysteries but could not complete them. It is my conviction that his social impulse is the foundation for the practical work of the new mystery school, and that its elements, spoken of in the previous chapter, are important to spiritual life as well.

When Steiner wrote about freeing the individual from the interests of associations in his Fundamental Sociological Law in 1898, he pointed to a turn in world history that was reached when Christ overcame death. From this moment on a new force became active in humanity. It was experienced in the spiritual rebirth of the first Whitsun festival, when the higher being of each individual was activated in community with others. When we experience our higher being as born within and giving our life direction, we do not need outside authority anymore. The spirit is active from the inside out.

This also means that any spiritual tutelage must cease. The turning point is the activation of our higher being. Other people can be midwives in this process, as we will see later.

Our higher being was not yet active in the old mysteries. People were under the authority of a teacher (or guru in the Indian tradition) and followed him completely. The ego was placed under the control of the teacher. The teacher's higher being came to expression in the student, who then tried to act out of the intentions of his teacher. Asian schools of inner development still use this form of teaching, but it can only lead to a rupture in the biography of the individual. The teacher had a different role on the Christian path of development in the Middle Ages. He was a mediator leading the student to Christ. Since the late Middle Ages a teacher on the Rosicrucian path became more and more a friend whose authority rested on inner acceptance. Steiner continued this direction of guidance by pointing to the trust relationship of teacher and student, and to our ability to judge when practicing spiritual exercises. The actual teacher lives in our heart. It is the Christ.

Steiner made another step seven years later when he formulated the Fundamental Social Law concerning the division of labor and income. He said that if this law was neglected a true conviction of reincarnation and karma could not thrive in the world. It is important that Steiner pointed to the practical meaning of spiritual science for social life when he formulated the law for the first time in 1905. The theosophical idea of brotherhood was to be realized in concrete social life.

The old mysteries took place in the seclusion of temples. The new mysteries are not bound to a certain place or time of meditation anymore. They take place in full life, in "social etheric" temples where spiritual life can be applied practically everywhere and at any time of day. In the past it was not a common practice to inquire about destiny or karmic ties, but in order to come to spiritual cognition and develop initiatives we must now ask these questions when we want to associate with others in spiritual life and in communities. That is why we need karma exercises.

The archetypal phenomenon of social life is the third element of the social impulse. It closely relates to what was said before, which is that we learn about the other in encounters and that we also get to know ourselves through the other. When we fall asleep in the other as listeners and take them into ourselves, they can awaken "in" us. We can then take into our soul and give back what they say out of our own inner experience. The receivers feel recognized and strengthened. Sometimes they receive a completely new perspective of themselves. Our higher being can awaken in a whole new way in encounters and new connections between people. From this experience new forms of community can arise that belong to the new mysteries. In the old mysteries encounters with others did not play the essential role they have today. At that time, above all, the relationship with the teacher was important.

With the impulse of social threefolding Rudolf Steiner made clear that social life becomes really human only when we create social forms, new communities where the other human being can develop in his or her own particular way. In terms of spiritual life this means that we consciously develop social forms where new mysteries can truly live: for example, forms where people can meet and awaken, and forms for group work and for building a new culture. This began with the Christmas Conference of 1923, and since then only continues in small circles. There are new social forms that also help us to maintain our forces of soul in a time when thinking, feeling and willing are increasingly separated. It is one of the reasons why a threefold social organism is necessary. We can then consciously experience the three different qualities of soul in the three subsystems of social life and integrate them out of the spiritual forces of our being.

In examining the meaning of the social impulse for spiritual life we discovered some fundamental aspects of the practical work Steiner wanted to initiate in the new mystery school. This work presupposes human freedom and an awakening consciousness of our higher being. It takes place where people participate in the world and want to help each other to realize their spiritual impulses in encounters and common initiatives. This work takes place in public so that everyone can take part out of one's own initiative. In contrast, the work in the old mystery schools was accessible only to the chosen. Modern humanity must consciously associate with others and ask questions with a deep human interest, as Percival did on his quest for the Grail. Then the spiritual world can reveal itself to us. How this can happen in a concrete form will be described later.

In the new mysteries Anthroposophy is no longer a worldview with its own dogmas that could be cultivated in a sect with its own language and subculture. It is a living perception of the spiritual world in our own soul. As higher spiritual consciousness, Anthroposophy wants to be born in the soul of individuals, and that process requires a deep inner transformation.

## 2. The Path to the New Mysteries

A force that renews the old layers of the soul has been active in the world since the mystery of Golgotha: "See, I make all things new." These are Christ's words from the Book of Revelation. This impulse can renew our life through the forces of our higher being because Christ dwells within. It was once mostly individual work, but now it can be carried more and more by others as well. The earth has been in a process of transformation since the Christ impulse, which is the impulse of love: "from cosmos of wisdom to cosmos of love," said Steiner. Cosmic wisdom lived in the old mysteries; the force of love lives in the new mysteries.

The wisdom of the mystery temples in Greek culture appeared in philosophy: literally meaning "love for wisdom". The 20th century witnessed a transition from philosophy to Anthroposophy, in which the mystery-wisdom becomes accessible again. Steiner spoke of the being of Sophia "Holy Wisdom", silenced and veiled when the old mysteries died. Since the end of the 19th century, she was awakened again by the Archangel Michael, to speak and be born out of the soul of human beings as Anthropo-Sophia, "wisdom of man". Steiner understood "Anthroposophy" as the consciousness of true humanity, the consciousness of the renewing force of Christ in the soul of each individual.

The Theosophical Society represented the stream of old mystery wisdom from Asia. Through Marie von Sivers' question, Steiner was able to bring the Christ impulse to the Theosophical Society and transform this old stream of wisdom into a stream of love. Love can be experienced as the fruit of wisdom reborn in the inner being of humanity; wisdom can transform into love only in the individual human soul. After the final break with the Theosophical Society in 1913, Steiner continued to prepare the new stream in the Anthroposophical Society. Once Ita Wegman – a physician, one who had been in contact with Steiner since the beginning of his theosophical times – posed her question, new mystery sciences could begin.

The question for a renewal of the mysteries was posed at a critical time. Steiner experienced intense attacks on Anthroposophy from the outside world in 1922. In Munich, he narrowly escaped a murder attempt by national socialists on May 5, 1922, and at the same time conflicts within the Anthroposophical Society appeared as well. Membership had grown since the end of the First World War. A bureaucratic apparatus in Stuttgart had begun to regulate the affairs of the society in a rather arbitrary way. Initiatives separated from the mother, the Anthroposophical Society.

On September 16, 1922, the Christian Community was founded in Stuttgart by a group of 45 theologians, pastors and students as a Movement for religious renewal. Many Anthroposophists, sometimes entire branches, became members of the new congregations, and Steiner soon had to say emphatically that the Christian Community had a task different from that of the Anthroposophical Society.

Inner conflicts were most difficult. One side saw older members of Theosophical times who often held little interest in the world, and had a rather sectarian attitude. On the other side, young people wanted to apply Anthroposophy practically with their will forces. They had as yet little spiritual depth. Among them were young academics like Walter Johannes Stein and Eugen Kolisko. They often brought their scientific thinking into Anthroposophy instead of renewing the sciences out of Anthroposophy. Other young people came from the German youth movement. For them Rudolf Steiner gave the *Pedagogical Course for Youth* in October 1922.[33]

In the midst of this crisis the wooden Goetheanum, the living center of the Anthroposophical movement in Dornach, burnt down on New Year's Eve 1922-23. It fell victim to arson by enemies of Anthroposophy. According to Steiner this could happen because the members were not awake enough and the Society had become inwardly hollow. The night of the fire saw a turn in the life of Ita Wegman, movingly described in a biography by Emanuel Zeylmans van Emmichoven. Wegman had been used to achieving everything out of her own strength, and for years had received Rudolf Steiner's help. However, during the fire she suddenly realized that no one seemed to care for his life's goals. At that moment she decided to devote herself unconditionally to his cause.

---

33  Rudolf Steiner, *Pedagogical Course for Youth*, Great Barrington 2007 (CW 217).

At the end of August, 1923, Steiner held a course in Wales. It was there that Ita Wegman asked him for a spiritual medical science as it had existed during the old mysteries. The initiates in the mystery temples had held great medical knowledge, and Wegman asked whether Anthroposophy could open this mystery wisdom with its scientific consciousness to modern humanity. Steiner agreed and answered that "mystery medicine" was to come to life again. Together they laid the foundation for Anthroposophical medicine through intense cooperation.

That same year Steiner sought to solve the crisis within the Society. He spoke of an "inner opposition "to his goals in early 1923, and at the end of February decided to found a new society parallel to the old one: The Free Anthroposophical Society, which was in existence until 1931. It was to serve young Anthroposophists and those who did not feel at home in the hierarchic society. It was headed by a committee including Hans Büchenbacher, Jürgen von Grone, Ernst Lehrs, René Maikowski, Wilhelm Rath, and Maria Röschl. By the end of 1925 this society had 1150 members.

National societies were founded in several countries, and Steiner waited to see what they intended with regards to the planned Christmas Conference. He even wrestled with the question of leaving the society to form an order with 48 (4x12) members. On November 17, 1923, he decided to become chairman of a new Anthroposophical Society, inaugurated in 1923 at the Christmas Conference. This was a great personal sacrifice. It was, in fact, an emergency solution that had personal consequences for himself as well.

This conference began to fulfill Rudolf Steiner's mission to found a new mystery culture carried by a community of practical people who took Anthroposophy into their souls. The new Society was to be the social organism where a new and conscious relationship to the spiritual world could be practiced in new mysteries. Steiner established the School for Spiritual Science. It was divided into sections with three classes where the new mysteries would be developed under his guidance. Everyone who wanted to represent Anthroposophy in the world could ask for admission into this school.

Steiner's teaching took place on three levels that we also find in other spiritual schools (for example with the medieval Cathars): An initial level of public lectures for interested persons. A second level for members of the Anthroposophical Society who want to study Anthroposophy, to develop their consciousness and to associate with other members. And a third level for members of the new mystery school, who want to work in the world within their initiatives and who prepare themselves for an initiation. This school was a metamorphosis of the Esoteric School that was led by Steiner between 1904 and 1914.

The 1923 Christmas Conference was a mystery act. The members in attendance accepted the goals and rules of the new Society. The first article of the statutes of this Society states it to be "an association of people whose will it is to nurture the life of the soul, both in the individual and in human society, on the basis of a true knowledge of the spiritual world." The members were asked to consciously place the Foundation Stone of this new Anthroposophical Society into their hearts in order to develop the inner strength to unite, in close cooperation with each other, the work in the world with the deepest spirituality. A spiritual Goetheanum was to be built in the world, Rudolf Steiner said in his closing words on January 1, 1924, stating "On this foundation stone the building is to be erected, the individual stones of which will be the work that is being done in all our groups by individuals out in the world." Often it is said that Steiner laid this Foundation Stone in the hearts of the participants of the Christmas Conference of 1923, but that's not what he said. People have to do it themselves, then they can become proactive in the world and become Michaelites.

For placing this Foundation Stone into the heart and for strengthening this foundation for the work in the world, Steiner gave the Foundation Stone Meditation. He called this meditation, accessible to all of humanity, the modern version of the old aphorism "Know Thyself." It asks the modern soul to know itself and transform itself into a Grail vessel for the higher individuality to be born and for new forces of life to be activated. On this Foundation Stone the members of the newly founded School for Spiritual Science should build, with the mantras of the class lessons, a spiritual temple in their souls, in which they would be able to experience the beings of the spiritual world.

The mantras of the class lessons of this Michael School build upon the Foundation Stone Meditation. After preparation, the meditator approaches the threshold of the spiritual world, where he encounters three animals representing negative soul forces. He or she then comes to the Guardian of the Threshold, a representative of the Archangel Michael. This guardian, who from now on will be their admonishing and advising companion, stands on the border between the sense world and the spirit world, and warns them of three animals rising from the abyss there. These are the enemies on the path of knowledge of modern man: the fear of the spirit, the mockery of spiritual knowledge and the laziness of thought. They live in people's will, feeling and thinking. Only with "knowledge bravery, a burning thirst for knowledge and creative knowledge" can the meditating human being cross the abyss and enter through the gate into the hall of the spirit temple. There spiritual beings appear, up to the highest sphere of the divine Trinity. To the extent of their inner development, the meditators can have a perception of the temple and of these beings. Working with the mantras is a preparatory way to initiation, in the stages of purification of the soul (before the threshold), enlightenment, and initiation. The real initiation may take place later.

In this inner spirit temple Anthroposophists can receive inspirations from the spiritual world. However, in order to make them effective on a larger scale, they also need a "social etheric" temple where, together with others, they may receive such inspirations to do the joint work. The spirit temple arises from the inner, individual work, and the social temple arises from the common social work on the basis of the Anthroposophical Social Impulse.

The inner work with the mantras is a spiritual activity, whereas the social work is an etheric activity in which people work together. In my view, connecting the inner spirit temples of individual persons with the social temple that arises in their group work requires a method of working on research questions which, in 1923, Steiner called the "reversed cult". This will be discussed in the next section. In the combination of inner and social activities, the etheric, astral and spiritual work support each other to create a mystery center, a spiritual Goetheanum, on the Foundation Stone.

Whitsun is the descent of the spirit into community. The 1923 Christmas Conference can be experienced as the founding of a community that receives a new, conscious relationship with the spiritual world in the name of a newly awakening humanity. Sophia "Holy Wisdom" wants to be born in individuals as Anthropo-Sophia for the spirit to become active in culture. This motif weaves through the entire Christmas Conference. Steiner appealed to the members to suffuse their heart with Anthropo-Sophia in order to carry the new spirit into the world.[34]

In this spirit of Whitsun, Anthroposophy can only be of the heart. It is the new Anthroposophy that, since 1923, is to speak the language of the world and be experienced inwardly. Neither theosophical mysticism nor the intellectual Anthroposophy of young scientists, were suitable; neither can help people to awaken. Only a spiritual consciousness that is alive in the heart can bring this about. Thoughts

---
34  Rudolf Steiner: *Die Weihnachtstagung zur Begründung der Allgemeinen Anthroposophischen Gesellschaft* (1923-1924), Dornach 1994 (CW 260).

have to find their way to the heart so that it begins to think, Steiner said. If we want to overcome materialism and awaken the inner life in others, we must develop an intelligence of the heart, an inner Sophia-force in this Michaelic time.

This is not how Anthroposophy developed after 1923. Soon Rudolf Steiner had to conclude that the new impulses were not put into action. A cognition of karma that should have led to a cooperation of people from the different karmic streams within the Society did not take place. In his book *Rudolf Steiner's Leidensweg* [The Ordeal of Rudolf Steiner] the German anthroposophist Gerhard von Beckerath collected several statements given by Steiner relating to this. In September 1923, he said to the lawyer Bruno Krüger: "The impulse of the Christmas Conference is shattered" and to the eurythmist Ina Schuurman: "The Christmas Conference failed."[35]

After Steiner's death in 1925, the circles around Marie Steiner von Sivers were convinced that the attempt to found a new mystery culture at the Christmas Conference had failed. They guarded the seeds of the new culture given by Steiner. Another gradually growing circle considered the Christmas Conference and the Foundation Stone Meditation to be an indestructible fount of inspiration from which to draw. This was always Ita Wegman's conviction.

## 3. Awakening "on" and "in" the Other

A process of awakening began in Ita Wegman when she and Rudolf Steiner, deeply shaken, watched the burning of the first Goetheanum shortly after midnight on January 1, 1923. This process concerns the essence of this section. An image of Steiner as human being arose in Ita Wegman; she saw how everyone called on him for help, but no one seemed to help him. Out of compassion and an awakening

---
35  Gerhard von Beckerath: *Rudolf Steiners Leidensweg*, Dornach 2011.

social impulse she decided to apply herself entirely to his intentions. Here and in later meetings, images of previous lives arose in her in which he had been her teacher as well. Steiner explained the karma alighting in her, described by Zeylmans van Emmichoven in his Wegman biography. In these conversations her spirit awakened more and more, and this enabled them to cooperate fully.

Through Wegman's questions about renewing the mysteries, Steiner could then tell her how he wanted to create the new society under his guidance. On November 17, 1923, when he was in doubt about this, she told him that he could not leave the Society on its own. Wegman's biography goes on to describe how Steiner got up, walked over to her, took her hands in his and said warmly: "Yes, if you help me, then I will dare to do it!"[36] It is clear from this picture that not even an initiate of modern times can accomplish his task without the cooperation of the other perceiving him and asking the appropriate question.

New possibilities for spiritual research arose for Steiner through this deep meeting and consequent cooperation with Ita Wegman. He pointed this out in 1924, in the cycle *True and False Paths in Spiritual Investigation*.[37] The last lectures of this cycle describe a new path of researching the outer world in cooperation with others in karmic community. According to Steiner, old initiates strongly resisted this path, as it was founded on the clear, objective thinking of modern natural science. It is the path of research for people who want to cognize the sphere of natural phenomena out of a common impulse. The cooperation of Steiner and Wegman showed that it needed a process revealing karmic connections. It is exemplary how Steiner and Wegman developed the beginnings of the new mystery medicine as partners on this path.

---

[36] Immanuel Zeylmans van Emmichoven: *Who Was Ita Wegman?*, Vol. 4, Spring Valley 1995-2009.

[37] Rudolf Steiner: *True and False Paths in Spiritual Investigation* (1924), London 1985 (CW 243).

Step by step Rudolf Steiner had prepared the path to the new mysteries by engaging the members of his society in a process of building a spiritual community. It was difficult to unite people with their individual spiritual ways to prepare the future culture of brotherhood. The abstract idea of brotherhood had to be made concrete. On November 23, 1905, during the time he formulated the Fundamental Social Law, Steiner spoke of completely new possibilities that could arise out of community building when individuals lived selflessly, drawing their strength not only from themselves but also from others. Higher beings can then descend into these associations to act through the individual.[38] This is the fundamental principle of the new mysteries: self-conscious people invite spiritual beings to help and inspire them to create a new culture. The old mysteries saw people as servants to these higher beings.

Around 1912, Steiner often spoke of compassion as a uniting force between people and of entering into the inner being of the other. What lives in the other can come to life within us. The other wants to be understood, and this provides an opportunity to develop a sense of brotherhood. In relation to this, Steiner later gave a modern version of Christ's words: "What you have understood of the least of my brothers, this you understood of me." This is given an encompassing perspective in the lecture *Love and its Meaning in the World* from December 17, 1912.[39] Here Steiner spoke about the essence of the impulse of love as sun-force in the human world and of the danger when the creative force of love cannot be active in spiritual science.

Around the time that the idea of social threefolding was formed, Steiner elaborated the development of qualities of soul for social life even more concretely. Modern people, he said, become increasingly lonely, and contacting others becomes more difficult. We must

---

38  Rudolf Steiner: *Die Welträtsel und die Anthroposophie* (1905- 1906), Dornach 1983 (CW 54).

39  Rudolf Steiner: *Erfahrungen des Übersinnlichen - Die Wege der Seele zu Christus* (1912), Dornach 1994 (CW 143).

develop an interest in others and consciously work on inter-human understanding. Communities where people live and work in brotherhood and prepare a new culture must be built.

In the fall of 1918 Steiner mentioned several times what we may concretely experience in meetings. On October 9, 1918, he pointed to the possibility of perceiving the image of the Godhead hidden within every human being. When we have a deep interest in the other, it instills a certain secret of their nature. Meetings can then become sacramental; its impulse comes from the sphere of angels.[40]

On December 7, 1918, Steiner indicated that social qualities develop when we interact, and that we can learn to allow a picture, an image, of the other to arise in us. It should not be a picture of sympathy or antipathy, but a shining, purified image that expresses the person. We can learn to develop these pictures by looking back on our life and contemplating people who played a certain role in it. When we experience another person as an image, we enrich our life of soul. We develop brotherhood in a very concrete sense when we carry others in our soul.[41]

In a lecture from December 12, 1918, which is also part of this volume, Steiner emphasized that social life must be consciously cultivated, and that the interest in others, formerly instinctive, must be consciously acquired. He called interest in another person the "fundamental nerve" of all social life. This interest bridges the abyss to the other. The archetypal phenomenon of communication, treated by Steiner in this lecture, can be consciously activated only out of true interest and a willingness to make room for the other.

It is impossible to develop solely out of our own strength. We would get stuck in egoism. Conversations can lead us to a further awakening, particularly if the archetypal phenomenon of communication is employed with a certain consciousness and the other perceives what

---

[40] Rudolf Steiner: *The Dead Are With Us* (1918), London 1985 (CW 182).

[41] Rudolf Steiner: *The Challenge of the Times* (1918), Spring Valley 1941 (CW 186).

lives in us. Then we gain understanding of ourselves and develop a consciousness of our higher being. Through contemplating our life we become aware of how many people contributed decisively to our development: as teacher, friend, inspirer and even enemy.

These people are the midwives of our higher being. We meet unconscious aspects of our higher being in people we associate with, and then can learn to own them. On December 27, 1918, Steiner said that our higher being is in all we meet outside and least within ourselves. It meets us from the outside, in karmic relationships.[42] These meetings allow us to experience the awakening of our higher being in daily life as a social process. Through the renewing force of Christ the transformation of the old human being into the new human being (the inner, spiritual being) gradually takes place in our relationships. This process brings self-consciousness and an inkling of what lies within as possibilities and tasks.

This brief awakening of the higher being in our soul may be called a "moment of Whitsun". It is the festival of the free individuality as well as of the community, the festival of the birth of a higher being in the individual soul and the birth of a new sociality. Spirit individualizes in our higher being as Spirit Self and this spirit is the same for all. We are truly social only in our higher being; it is important to allow it to be born gradually, in concrete living and working together. This process must be supported by work on our soul.

In the crisis situation of the Anthroposophical Society of 1922 and 1923, Steiner tried to bridge the differences between the various groups by indicating a path to community building, the path to a new society. The new mysteries cannot function without being carried by a community. Many Anthroposophists lacked the experience of community in the Anthroposophical Society and turned to the Christian Community, the Movement for religious renewal founded in 1922. Steiner wanted to show them that Anthroposophy has its

---

42  Rudolf Steiner: *How Can Mankind Find the Christ Again?* (1918-1919), Hudson 1984 (CW 187).

own way of community building and described it in the lectures of February 27 and March 3, 1923.[43]

Steiner pointed out that people have had an elementary need to awaken "on" the spirit and soul [Erwachen am Geistig-Seelischen] of others since the beginning of the 20th century. He meant by this that we can awaken in the experience of the soul and the spirit of others. It is an increasing need to awaken "on" the deepest inner being of another to higher consciousness, a heightened waking consciousness. People must draw nearer to each other. They must become awakening people who can awaken the higher being in the other. Steiner said in these lectures that this is essential for Anthroposophy. If people cannot awaken to higher consciousness "on" another, they cannot yet truly understand Anthroposophy, nor will they be able to understand each other.

When we gather in the attitude of spiritual idealism to talk about spiritual ideas and to experience them, when we suffuse these ideas with our feeling with enthusiasm and impulses of will, "then can we awaken through each other," Rudolf Steiner said. A person may say something about a theme that occupies us as well. We hear something new. Another sheds light on the subject in an entirely new way. We discover what has long been slumbering but could not yet be expressed until another starts to speak, or because of their speaking, we are inspired to deeds in which we create new karma with others.

Steiner also said that in this state of awakening "on" another we lift ourselves with our life of soul into a supersensible sphere and can experience how a spiritual being descends on us. We are then united in a spiritual community. This is an experience of community where a spiritual being unites us. Steiner spoke of a "reversed cult" (or "reverse ritual"), a "knowledge cult" in which the participants pursue insight. In such a conversation they can

---

43  Rudolf Steiner: *Awakening To Community* (1923), Hudson 1974 (CW 257).

consciously experience their thoughts and feelings being lifted to the supersensible world.

In this process of awakening the head can connect with the heart, which is important for the member groups of the Society as well as for the work in the sections of the School for Spiritual Science. After all, the goal of the "knowledge cult" has not yet been exhausted in the process of community building. For who is the spiritual being uniting people in a spiritual community? This seems to me to be the being who is connected with the specific group that regularly comes together. This being can inspire them and through this being other spiritual beings can also give insights to the group.

This contrasts with the cult of Christian churches, such as the Christian Community. Here, Steiner said, the cult community creates conditions for angels to descend into the cultic space and to unite the assembled congregation into a community. The experience of community with spiritual beings is very different in these two ways of community building (spiritual work and participating in a religious cult). The Christian cult provides an experience of community as a gift from above through the mediation of a priest and inner activity of the congregation. In spiritual work, the participants in a conversation have to achieve this from below to above, in the "knowledge cult", by working with spiritual contents in the common process of cognition. Here the cult community and the cognition community stand side by side. As a third form we can add the social community. So we can distinguish three forms of community formation:

1. The formation of a religious community: The cultic community arises in the celebration of the religious service as the descending angelic beings give the community a communal experience. Cultic activities work on a "social etheric" level.

2. The formation of an Anthroposophical community: This cognition community arises in the "knowledge cult" in that the participants in a conversation about spiritual ideas awaken to each other, spiritually rising to a supersensible sphere, and a spiritual being unites them in a spiritual community.
3. The formation of a social community: This community emerges in social life on the basis of the Anthroposophical Social Impulse, which prepares the community life of the Slavic culture of the future.

We can remark here that the Christian Community is not only a cultic community, but also wants to develop itself in social life as a congregation. For that reason the Anthroposophical Social Impulse is also highly relevant for the development of the Christian Community.

Since the Christmas Conference of 1923 Anthroposophists must cooperate to create the foundations for a new culture where concrete communities arise in which the spiritual world can reveal itself. Spiritual knowledge was previously revealed to individuals, to initiates. This path of revelation out of the sphere of God the Father, from above to below, gradually ceases. Since 1899, the end of Kali Yuga, this is replaced by a path from below to above. This path begins with awakening "on" the other and leads to higher consciousness in the "knowledge cult", to the awakening of our inner self. We can work with spiritual contents on this path and develop our forces of soul.

This cultivation of the life of soul can be deepened when we talk about these contents and what they awaken in us. Then our life of soul is brought to consciousness and order, and the inner Self is further awakened. This is no longer in the sphere of the Father God, but in the sphere of the Son. Christ transforms the soul and takes part in the process of individualization. He can also affect the birth of a new inner man where groups cultivate the life of soul. These groups must be a home for soul and spirit that everyone likes to attend, where people can learn about others through discussing spiritual topics, experiencing joy and getting to know themselves. These member groups should be small for transformations to take place.

It is rather common to read cycles of Steiner's lectures in Anthroposophical circles, but if we do not cultivate the life of soul it rather hardens when we mechanically repeat his ideas and refer to his authority. The topic (It need not be a book, but can also be a phenomenon of the times) should spark conversation. We can talk about our spiritual experiences and our personal relationship to the subject. This has been customary in many spiritual circles since the 1970s. In a spirit of tolerance, each person can contribute to the topic and the thoughts of others and take what was said into his feeling and willing. In 1923 Steiner frequently pointed out that the artistic as well as religious experiences must be addressed: why should member groups not sing together, practice Eurythmy, paint, play music or perform a theatre play together and in this way experience moments of soul development? On January 1, 1923, Steiner said that Anthroposophy begins with science and its ideas come to life in the arts, ending with religious deepening.[44] Then Anthroposophy takes hold of the entire soul.

The work in some member groups is still rather traditional. The members remain strangers to each other, only a few speak (usually men) and thoughts remain abstract and uncommitted. The "knowledge cult" does not take place there. Anthroposophy could learn a lot about group work and transformational processes of the soul from modern psychology. Steiner also suggested to young members of the already mentioned Free Anthroposophical Society to tell each other about their lives and to karmically associate.

---

44  Ibid.

Some young people, among them Wilhelm Rath and Ernst Lehrs, were inspired by the circle of the Friends of God from the Bernese Oberland (Switzerland), who gathered around the then reincarnated Master Jesus in the 14th century. They asked Steiner in October 1922 for a meditative content for their inner work. This led to the Esoteric Youth Circle, for which Steiner also gave two esoteric lessons. Among the twelve founding members were Daniel van Bemmelen, Herbert Hahn, Ernst Lehrs, René Maikowski and Wilhelm Rath. This independent meditation community still exists today and is usually called The Circle.[45]

Steiner also told these young people that they should talk about their spiritual experiences. When they replied that that did not have such experiences, he answered that they had them every day. They should also become friends. This advice he could not give to the elder members. They were used to the traditional ways of the branches of the Theosophical Society that Steiner wanted to fundamentally transform. However, due to his death this was not possible.

A century ago people did not like to talk about what went on in their soul. Today we live in a different time and are much more direct. Young people are less restrained. We want to know who the other is, why they feel connected to Anthroposophy, how they live, and what they experience and read. This is also true for topics that were never discussed at other times. Contact has become less formal than what was common in Anthroposophical circles. In spiritually oriented groups, meetings and relationships can be much deeper now on the human social level. Here begins the social path of community building with the social impulse of Anthroposophy.

This process brings the inter-human association out of the strict sphere of ideas, and it begins to take hold of the soul. We enter the personal lives and destinies of others when deep meetings take place, and we try to work together and order mutual karma, like

---

45  Benjamin Schmidt: *Wilhelm Rath,* Stuttgart 2018.

Steiner and Wegman. We may discover that we have a positive or negative common karma from the past and may need to clean up a bit. Or we may have to solve some mutual problems first in order to build up forward-looking karma (e.g. because we don't like each other or because certain characteristics and aspects of the double of others bother us).

Conversations acquire different qualities to the degree that we succeed in consciously applying the archetypal phenomenon of communication. When we can truly listen, the other can awaken "in" us on a higher level. They can find themselves. When I speak and the other consciously falls asleep in me, I can awaken "in" the other. This is takes place in encounters. When a conversation takes place in a group of friends, in a member group or in a research group we can experience an awakening "on" the other in which our consciousness is broadened in the practice of the "knowledge cult". In encounters and in group conversations, a new sphere may open for participants in deep conversation; it is the Whitsun sphere of the Holy Spirit, the sphere of the new mysteries.

When a person can speak in my space of consciousness and he or she awakens "in" me, I allow myself to be filled by their higher being. I can gain deep insight into what lives in them, and sometimes hear more than what they say and are conscious of. If I am receptive and able to hold it, I can give it back and offer it to their consciousness. This process can be mutual, and a deep meeting can thus mutually bring our spirits to activity from the inside. On this path a meeting can indeed become a sacrament. We can experience a moment of Whitsun, the moment of living in community with the spiritual world.

This kind of conversation does not only allow awakening each other, it can also provide answers to questions of the times or to problems. Rudolf Steiner and Ita Wegman experienced the spiritual world revealing itself and giving answers in conversations they held on medical questions. We need not be initiates to receive these answers in a group. New, surprising aspects of communication with regards to the activity of Christ in meetings and conversations are described by Marjorie Spock in her studies on Goethean conversation, and Margarete van den Brink in her book *More Precious than Light*.[46] Steiner even said once that a group can replace the initiate.

In conversation and cooperation, we can create a supersensible, social space with the forces of our heart. We can build a "social etheric" temple for spiritual beings to descend and the spiritual world to reveal itself. People cooperating in research who can receive revelations from the spiritual world complete the path of cognition begun in a conversation on spiritual ideas. Through the further development of consciousness, group conversations hold the same possibilities as a conversation between two people. The old path of revelation from the sphere of the Father God can then be replaced by a new path of revelation where common research can draw spiritual knowledge out of the sphere of the Holy Spirit.

The practical work in the new mysteries is built upon processes of awakening that lead us from individual paths to social paths. Individual awakening takes place when we broaden our consciousness in conversation about spiritual contents, and when we associate compassionately, through interest and love and through creating images of the other. We can support this by following an individual path of developing our soul forces, our self-consciousness and our moral consciousness, and of opening the organs to perceive the spiritual world. Individual exercises and the class lessons of the School for Spiritual Science can be helpful. But altogether new possibilities arise when we add a social path of development to the individual path; when we learn to consciously apply the archetypal phenomenon of communication, have deep meetings with others,

---

[46] Marjorie Spock: *Group Moral Artistry (I. Reflections on Community Building: II. The Art of Goethean Conversation)*, Spring Valley 1983. Margarete van den Brink: *More Precious Than Light - How Dialogue Can Transform Relationships and Build Community*, Stroud 1996.

gradually order mutual karma and form a community. Then social impulses awaken. This social path will be elaborated later on.

Cultivating the life of soul, when we place the soul forces in the light of consciousness and allow them to be transformed, is fundamental to our awakening. This activates our consciousness soul (the self-conscious soul), which has two aspects that need to be united. The male aspect of the consciousness soul is well known. It relates to clear thinking, objectivity, goal orientation, sense for the practical, strength of judgment and action. It is focused to the outside and unites thinking and willing. The female aspect is focused more to the inside and builds forces of heart, such as receptivity, reverence, devotion, gentleness, humility, service, and intelligence of heart. Through this aspect we can associate with the outer world in love, take it into ourselves, and understand another human being from the inside, possibly even better than he or she would be able to express in words.

The male aspect lives in the process of awakening. We lift ourselves into a supersensible sphere, but the spiritual world cannot reveal itself without help from the female aspect. We must be able to fall asleep and become receptive for what lives in the others as a mysterious tone in the conversation. What reveals itself must be expressed in words by the male forces of cognition again, brought to consciousness and understood by each person. Spiritual conversation with the higher worlds lives in this alternation of falling asleep and awakening, perceiving and thinking, sensing and understanding, with Logos and Sophia forces.

Logos forces are the forces of speech through which our consciousness opens for others and ourselves. In contrast to these male Michaelic forces of our consciousness soul, Sophia forces of our consciousness soul are female. They are the intelligence of the heart, the inner wisdom that is our organ of receiving the spiritual world. Steiner called the spiritualized consciousness soul the "Sophia in us" (in esoteric Christianity: the "Virgin Sophia"). Anthropo-Sophia comes to life in us to the degree we develop these Sophia and Logos forces.

The Platonists and Aristotelians, often mentioned in Anthroposophy, can be understood as representatives of these female and male forces. According to Rudolf Steiner, the Platonists of the School of Chartres and the great Aristotelians of the late Middle Ages agreed to work together at the end of the 20th century to spiritualize human intelligence. This means that our materialistic intelligence can reconnect with the spiritual world so that it can become spiritual again. For this purpose the male thinking with the head and the female thinking with the heart must connect with each other. Most people are unilaterally developed in this and are in their own way a Platonist or an Aristotelian.

What I mean here are kinds of soul, not the relatively small number of members from the schools of Plato and Aristotle in Antiquity, nor the later Christian and Muslim philosophers who were inspired by them. Platonists, as a kind of soul, come from the sphere of the old mysteries of the Father God. They have a natural openness to the spiritual world and a tendency to mysticism; this can be transformed by self-consciousness and confronting practical life. They often live in a subjective world and do not like to work with groups. It is important for them to make their inner world objective with the help of male forces of consciousness. The Aristotelian type of soul lives in the process of thinking and seeks to enter the spiritual world. They can get stuck in intellectualism and neglect to link their thinking with female forces of the heart. Not until they achieve this link can their soul open to the forces of Sophia and create room for revelations from the sphere of the Holy Spirit. In order to realize the new mysteries, they have to work together with the Platonic types of soul in the Anthroposophical movement.

By working with people with the other soul quality, we can be encouraged to further develop this quality within ourselves as well.

These two soul types are present in everybody, but they are not equally strong. It is all about harmonizing them. This connection of head and heart is a task for everyone.

The new mysteries lead to new ways of research that arise out of community: ways of researching the outer world, as shown by Steiner and Wegman, and of researching the inner and social world. These paths of research are open to two people as well as groups. In a group setting the higher beings of the participants associate in the social space and one person can speak certain intuitions for the whole group who can receive them like a vessel. Revelations that previously were only given to initiates can again be received in social life.

On January 6, 1924, Steiner described how seven members of the late-medieval Rosicrucian brotherhood gathered in their meditation room. Three of them received certain symbolic revelations from the spiritual world that had to be interpreted by the other four.[47] Here we see the female and male qualities of consciousness cooperating to prepare the new mysteries. These circles build brotherhood in cognition where one person depends on the other. The Rosicrucians experienced how the spiritual world became inaccessible to consciousness. Four centuries later Rudolf Steiner and Ita Wegman were able to create a modern mystery medicine as modern Rosicrucians in the ebb and flow of objective conversation.

If we want to enter the new mysteries and work with others we need groups that cultivate the life of soul and support our processes of awakening. We must not only learn to awaken, but also be able to consciously fall asleep into the other as well. We need to understand the male and female forces of consciousness, as they often collide in group-settings, and to integrate them into our consciousness soul. In this way, Anthroposophy can come to life, not merely as thought in a male way or experienced in a female way. This care

---

[47] Rudolf Steiner: *Mysterienstätten des Mittelalters* (1924), Dornach 1991 (CW 233a).

for the soul is the task of member groups of the Anthroposophical Society. Then Anthroposophy can incarnate in the present and find the appropriate language in conversations between spiritually awakened people. Then the new mysteries can be realized gradually in concrete areas of work, and help solve the questions of our time though conversations where people open their soul to the spirit.

In 1923, the Anthroposophical Society was still on its way to these new mysteries. Steiner asked for ordering karma and building community. The members' attention was strongly focused to the inside, to their own awakening. We are called to action when out of a social impulse we begin to discover that the others need us in order to awaken. Ita Wegman discovered that in the night the Goetheanum burned.

Now we can summarize the difference between the different paths of community building. The community building of the Christian Community is a religious path that is often seen as a path that is not for Anthroposophists, who have their own cognition path to community. This separation should, however, not be considered absolute. At the end of 1922 it was necessary for Steiner to distinguish between the goals of the Anthroposophical Society and the Christian Community. In Peter Deunov's School of the White Brotherhood there is no such distinction between the religious, the cognitive and the social aspects of spiritual life.

The path of the knowledge community combines male and female approaches. One part is a male, Michaelic, Aristotelian path of posing questions and doing research. It has as its counterpart the path of listening and receiving spiritual insights, which is a female, Sophianic, Platonic path giving space to revelations from the spiritual world. These male and female paths belong together; they are complementary and both necessary for the knowledge cult.

The path of social community building is a path of overcoming individualism and of making space for others, as is shown by the

Social Impulse of Anthroposophy. This social impulse also dismantles old structures and makes room for social renewal. This brings us to the question of how Steiner wanted to renew the Anthroposophical Society, and how the Society took up this impulse of renewal. The destiny of the Society is exemplary, as many spiritual movements make an attempt to transform old forces and free new impulses.

## 4. The Destiny of the Society

Today's common perspectives are reversed by the social impulse. We should not be primarily concerned with our own development anymore, but with the development of the other. The questions of the times are essential, not what we personally consider important group work. Ita Wegman asked Rudolf Steiner the decisive question, and it revealed what lived in him as impulse, and thus began the new mysteries. In order to participate in these mysteries, we must bring about this reversal of perspective within and experience an inner transformation.

More and more people want to join this process. In the 1920s it predominantly took place in the sphere of ideas, in a frame of hierarchy and authority. People wanted to awaken "on" each other in the world of ideas, and in this way they experienced a broadening of consciousness and sense of community. Today we seek meetings and situations of equality and a direct relationship with the other and their experiences instead of being distanced through listening to their ideas. This turning to concrete meetings with others with whom we want to work together is characteristic of the new mysteries.

At the Christmas Conference of 1923, Steiner developed social forms for the newly founded Anthroposophical Society. This should make a new and conscious relationship to the spiritual world possible and replace the old bureaucratic society. In the old society, the around 12,000 members had a difficult time with each other. Their spiritual life took place in the seclusion of private life. Steiner wanted to create the "freest and most modern society possible", in which the Anthroposophical movement (here in the sense of the Michael movement in the spiritual world) should find its home.

The structure Rudolf Steiner intended to create was an expression of threefolding, with the new Anthroposophical Society as the social sphere, the School for Spiritual Science as the spiritual life, and an administrative society for practical matters. He never clearly expressed his intentions, but they can be deduced from his actions:

1. The Anthroposophical Society represented the inter-human sphere, the sphere of the soul, the heart of the social organism of Anthroposophy. All members are equal and can begin new activities out of their meetings with others. They want "to nurture the life of the soul". According to the statutes, this society was to further research in the spiritual field.
2. The School for Spiritual Science was to develop the spiritual life of the new mysteries. Here spiritual research could take place.
3. In February 1925 the existing Goetheanum Society was given the name General Anthroposophical Society. It was restructured in such a way that Steiner, as its first president, could represent to the outside world the Anthroposophical institutions that had emerged from the Anthroposophical movement.

Steiner discussed the statutes of the Anthroposophical Society during the Christmas Conference with the attending members; they were accepted in the third reading. These statutes are unusual because Steiner wanted to exclude anything pointing to an official society. It was not concerned with fixing the usual contents, but with a description of how the relationship from person to person and executive to members is envisioned, as well as with the intentions of the executive. Anything administrative was left out. Nothing could interfere in the Society's life with these statutes. Anyone who considered the existence of the Goetheanum as a School for Spiritual Science as justified could become a member and experience its way of cultivating the life of soul. No one's freedom was curbed.

Steiner wanted to found the freest, most modern society, and expected hundreds of thousands: indeed, millions, of people to join. The first Executive Council was not elected or nominated but formed in agreement with the members. It was to develop initiative, make available to members what it considered important, and assist them through advising and inspiring. The members were free to do what they considered right. They could develop a personal Anthroposophy without obligation to an authority and in cooperation with people they wanted to associate with for that purpose. Expulsion was impossible because no one may presume to judge the inner connection one person or another has to Anthroposophy.

That was different in the School for Spiritual Science. Here one was under the authority of Rudolf Steiner, and it was possible to be excluded. Everybody could apply for membership after having studied Anthroposophy seriously for two years. Steiner intended to establish three classes:

- The first class for an unlimited number of members who took Anthroposophy seriously and wanted to associate with it inwardly under Ita Wegman's guidance
- The second class, with 36 members, including leaders of the sections, lecturers and others, under the guidance of Marie Steiner-von Sivers
- The third class, with 12 members (the esoteric board of the Society), guided by himself

Steiner indicated this in a conversation with Ludwig Polzer-Hoditz on November 11, 1924.[48] He partly built the first class with nineteen so-called class lessons.

At the Christmas Conference Steiner announced establishing a relationship between the Anthroposophical Society's executive and the Johannesbau Association, which existed since 1911, built the first Goetheanum and prepared the building of the second. In 1918 this building association was renamed the Goetheanum Society. In three different attempts this society was transformed into the legal carrier of the four most important Anthroposophical institutions. It was to administer Marie Steiner's publishing house, Ita Wegman's clinic, the Anthroposophical Society, and the rebuilding of the Goetheanum. It received the name General Anthroposophical Society (GAS) and was registered on March 3, 1925, with statutes established on February 8, 1925.

The Society of the Christmas Conference of 1923 (AS) was not officially registered. As will be explained below, misunderstandings became apparent on 8 February, 1925. Emanuel Zeylmans van Emmichoven has clarified this background in the third volume of his Wegman biography.[49]

The administrative Society (GAS), sharing an identical executive with the spiritual Society (AS), had very different statutes. As administrative body it obviously had a limited number of members able to vote. They administered on the basis of their expertise. Members unable to find their way into the concordant administrative activity of others could be excluded. People contributing with donations could ask for membership but did not have the right to vote. This was reserved for the members proper. Shortly before his death Steiner

---

48  T.H. Meyer: *Ludwig Polzer-Hoditz, A European*, London 2014, part 6.

49  J.E. Zeylmans van Emmichoven: *Who Was Ita Wegman?*, Introduction to Vol. 3.

nominated seven administrators to the administrative Society; they never had a chance to act because confusion soon set in.

From the Christmas Conference on, Rudolf Steiner could freely speak about laws of karma, and positive and negative links of destiny that had arisen between groups in the Society in the past. He hoped that this might help solve open and latent conflicts within. Above all, the conflicts were between members who were interested in spiritual knowledge and younger members who wanted to apply the Anthroposophical impulses. There were heavy tensions between Marie Steiner von Sivers and Ita Wegman, who represented these two groups.

Steiner soon discovered that the members did not take up the impulse of the new mysteries. The Christmas Conference had failed, he said to several people, as Gerhard von Beckerath documented in his already mentioned book. The awakening, necessary to order and reconcile old karma (moon-karma) and begin new links of destiny that point to the future (sun-karma) did not take place.

Emanuel Zeylmans wrote: "His [Steiner's] disappointment that his presentations of the karma of his closest collaborators in the Anthroposophical Society and his suggestion to do karma exercises had not been taken up by those concerned was great; he indicated to Wegman that this would mean that he would no longer be able to work in the Society."[50]

Steiner's "Letters to the Members" (January until August 1924), written after the Christmas Conference, were meant to inspire them to make the new impulses effective.[51] Anthroposophy has to live in the hearts of people; each time a person speaks it can be born anew. Members have to find the paths from soul to soul in living interest for each other. People have to meet and share Anthroposophy as it

---

50  J.E. Zeylmans van Emmichoven: *Who Was Ita Wegman?*, Vol. I.

51  Rudolf Steiner: "Letters to the Members," in: Die Konstitution der Allgemeinen Anthroposophischen Gesellschaft und *der Freien Hochschule für Geisteswissenschaft. Der Wiederaufbau des Goetheanum* (1924-1925), Dornach 1987 (CW 260a).

lives in their soul. The Society has to be open for people to freely enter and get to know Anthroposophy. To further the awakening of people on and in each other Steiner wanted to re-create the closed branches from the theosophical time into open member groups where people can discover the intentions and tasks of their life. What is read or listened to can cause the further development of the life of soul of the individual.

The burning of the first Goetheanum a year earlier had already weakened Steiner's etheric body. He was able to recover his strength after the poisoning within a few hours, but remained very vulnerable. A further attack on his health followed at the end of the Christmas Conference, on January 1, 1924. He was poisoned, apparently on the orders of Western occultists, who possibly also had to do with Steiner's later illness, as Ehrenfried Pfeiffer discovered.[52]

By becoming president of the Society after the Christmas Conference, Steiner became responsible for what members did as Anthroposophists. More and more people came to him with their personal problems and exhausted him. He did not want to disappoint anyone despite the enormous strain he was exposed to following the Christmas Conference. According to Steiner the members had nine months to take up the new impulse. This did not happen. On September 28, 1924, Steiner held his last lecture. He had come to the end of his strength.

For Ita Wegman, Rudolf Steiner's illness was a consequence of "the fact that his impulses with regard to the Christmas Conference were not sufficiently taken up," "Then karma will work." Steiner had told her.[53] He had warned that the impulse of the Christmas Conference could evaporate. During the course of his illness he still hoped that the members would wake up. They did not, and before the end

---

52  Thomas Meyer, *Milestones*, Basel 2015, chapter 21.

53  J.E. Zeylmans van Emmichoven: *Who Was Ita Wegman?*, Vol. I.

of his life the intended threefold structure of the Society's social organism was even undermined.

After finally establishing the statutes of the administrative General Anthroposophical Society on February 8, 1925, with Steiner's signature on the application for registration, it became apparent that no one understood that this Society differed from the spiritual Society founded at the Christmas Conference. The members of the latter were poorly informed about the existence of the administrative Society and Steiner's closest co-workers were still much too familiar to think in unitary structures where spiritual life is an administrative affair as well.

On February 8, 1925, it became clear how deeply asleep the people around Steiner still were in the sphere of social creation. Vice President Albert Steffen, thought that every member of the Society after the Christmas Conference could now vote on the affairs of the administrative Society. This is shown by an entry in his diary on February 9, 1925, included in the documents of GA260a.[54] The registered statutes state this fact only for the 15 members proper.

On March 22, 1925, a report was given to the members of the Anthroposophical Society, founded at the Christmas Conference, about this meeting of the executives of the General Anthroposophical Society.[55] Steiner did not write it; it was written by the Executive Council of the General Anthroposophical Society. The report stated that the four already mentioned institutions were integrated in the General Anthroposophical Society. The members must have thought that it was the new Society of the Christmas Conference, and that the four institutions were now included in this spiritual Society. The suggestion was altogether misleading. For the Executive Council now only the administrative General Anthroposophical

---

54  Rudolf Steiner: *Die Konstitution der Allgemeinen Anthroposophischen Gesellschaft und der Freien Hochschule für Geisteswissenschaft.* CW 260a).

55  Ibid., p. 567.

Society registered on 8 February existed. The spiritual Society with its statutes was put out of action.

This report from March 22, 1925, prepared the disappearance of the spiritual Society founded at the Christmas Conference of 1923. On March 30, 1925, Steiner retreated from earthly life quite unexpectedly, as Ita Wegman described on April 19, 1925 (included in her letters *An die Freunde* [To the Friends]).[56] The remaining members of the executive council were entirely unprepared and inexperienced for their new task and unable to unanimously rescue the new impulse. Immediately after the cremation of Steiner there was a heated argument between Ita Wegman and Marie Steiner von Sivers about the urn with his ashes. It is incomprehensible that esoterically trained people provoked demonic powers, then and later, that poisoned the "social etheric" space. They simply did not have the competency to solve conflicts and to heal their relationships.

Without Rudolf Steiner, the Society would no longer be viable in its former form. Already at the beginning of April 1925 Marie Steiner wanted to withdraw from the board. Albert Steffen announced in January 1926 that he wanted to found a Rudolf Steiner Society in order to save the Anthroposophical Society and the work of Rudolf Steiner.

During the Christmas days of 1925 a meeting of the General Anthroposophical Society (GAS) was held, to which all members of the Society founded at the Christmas meeting of 1923 (AS) were invited. They had become members of the administrative Society, which had quite different statutes. From the lack of understanding of those concerned at the time, the misunderstanding arose that today's Society is identical to the Anthroposophical Society of the Christmas Conference.

The German lawyer Manfred Leist admitted in a report from 1989 that the members of the Society of the Christmas Conference

---

56  Ita Wegman: *An die Freunde,* Arlesheim 1968.

1923 became members of a different Society two years later without being aware of it, but seemingly in "active participation".[57] This was based on the report of March 22, 1925. In 2001, however, two other lawyers concluded that there had not been a merger. The spiritual Society had never met after the Christmas Conference of 1923. It disappeared from the consciousness of its members and after Rudolf Steiner's death was only to be found in the spiritual world.

In 1925, the Anthroposophists had become members of an administrative society with other statutes, which only became accessible to members in 1935. The unfit statutes were adjusted in several steps, but its essential points remain contrary to the original statutes that are called principles today, something that cannot be due to their factual character. Conflicts and fights over power among members led to expulsions, an impossibility in the spiritual Society. The administrative Society's statutes contained a paragraph on expulsion, and it was used when the conflicts in the Executive Council blazed up so much after Steiner's death that demons had free reign and were able to tear the Society apart.

This complete darkening of consciousness took place on April 14, 1935, during a general members' meeting, in the course of which Ita Wegman and Elisabeth Vreede were expelled from the Executive Council, and together with the entire Dutch and English Anthroposophical Societies and the German working groups excluded from the General Anthroposophical Society. Only Ludwig Polzer-Hoditz had the presence of mind and courage at this general meeting to openly speak against these exclusions and remind everyone of the intentions of the Christmas Conference 1923. His words expressed the great tragedy of a society that can only live spiritually between

---

57  Manfred Leist: "Zur Konstitution der Anthroposophischen Gesellschaft", in: Was in der Anthroposophischen Gesellschaft vorgeht, *Das Goetheanum,* issue 66, Nr. 7, February 12, 1989, supplement for members.

people and had now turned entirely earthly. This speech was published in the biography of Polzer-Hoditz.[58]

Alongside Ita Wegman, who had severed her clinic from the General Anthroposophical Society already in 1931, other representatives of the new mysteries disappeared as well. In 1924 the new impulses had not been taken up, and at Rudolf Steiner's death, the mysteries were veiled again. The Society took the path back to old forms of spiritual life. This could only lead to a presently unjust exertion of power in spiritual life and a violation of human freedom and dignity, to expulsion without reasons given, for example. The bureaucratic apparatus usurped spiritual life and the double (the dark shadow spirit taking power in a group or society when consciousness weakens) appeared in the Society, expelling the living spirit of Anthroposophy.

This should not surprise us. Sociology considers it a normal phenomenon when spiritual life enters a process of institutionalization and bureaucratization. When the inspiring teacher disappears, battles over power arise among students, and routine takes the place of enthusiasm. It took place in all spiritual streams, including Christianity. Steiner wanted to prevent this by creating a threefold social organism for the new mystery school. On February 28, 1923, he explained why this was needed: "We unite on the ground of spiritual science by differentiating and individualizing, not by centralizing."[59] A spiritual movement can then avoid the described sociological process.

Steiner strongly resisted several tendencies he perceived in the Society, even before the Christmas Conference. They were centralism, a one-sided male intellectual approach to Anthroposophy, and hierarchical thinking. Since his death these tendencies increasingly showed up. The heart of the threefold organism, the sphere of

---

58  T.H. Meyer: *Ludwig Polzer-Hoditz, A European,* London 2014, part 6.

59  Rudolf Steiner: *Das Schicksalsjahr* 1923, Dornach 1991 (CW 259).

cultivation of the soul, of meeting and also of rights where we face each other as equals, disappeared when the administrative Society took over the spiritual Society. The sphere of the living Christ, active among people and taking part in their processes of development vanished. This element of social life is very vulnerable, and is everywhere gradually destroyed by modern technocracy. In a following step the General Anthroposophical Society received a completely unitary structure when President Albert Steffen was instructed at a members' meeting to become the leader of the School for Spiritual Science after the Second World War. Steiner did not assign a successor, as it was his duty alone to do so. In this way another step to a technocratic administration was made.

Steffen and Wachsmuth were to administrate the sections of the School with Elisabeth Vreede, according to a communication of Steiner to Polzer-Hoditz on November 11, 1924.[60] After the expulsion of Wegman and Vreede they had now the entire Society in their hands. They kept Marie Steiner von Sivers out of the affairs of the Executive Council as well. The Council became exclusively male while it originally consisted equally of men and women.

From notes made by Polzer-Hoditz after a meeting with Steiner on March 3, 1925, we understand that Steiner had chosen this parity in order to paralyze Jesuitism, which he strongly perceived at work in the Society.[61] Jesuitism is not limited to the order of Jesuits, a stream fighting the spirit and excluding the female element (the cultivation of the soul and living experience of the spiritual). The old Roman attitude of power continues in this stream. It is perceptible when people want to control and assess, judge and exclude in spiritual life. For example, in an Executive Council that decides who is a true Anthroposophist and which initiatives may be called "Anthroposophical." The old hierarchy then takes over power.

---

60   T.H. Meyer: *Ludwig Polzer-Hoditz, A European*, London 2014, part 6.
61   Ibid.

The impulse leading to the new mysteries was now reversed in all aspects. The new Society would leave members free to decide what to accept from the Executive Council. In reverse, the executives then wanted to decide what the members must do. The center would come to life in the new Society when the periphery (member groups) would activate the heart by its activity. It is reversed when the center considers itself the pump bringing the whole apparatus into movement. We find the same in the undoing of text publications announced by Rudolf Steiner at the Christmas Conference, and in other things such as the fact that until the 1990s the Executive Council considered itself an esoteric board and ran the School for Spiritual Science without having the spiritual and esoteric competence that only Steiner could claim.

From 1925 on, after the new spiritual impulses had been reversed, lodge-like structures arose in which a higher ranking person knew more than those beneath and was able to execute power. The Society lost its connection to the spiritual world and Anthroposophy could not freely stream into the world anymore. Thinking became a matter of the "right method", the heart forces were blocked and the will forces of the Anthroposophical movement were paralyzed.

Three fatal tendencies: the arising unitary structure, exclusion of the female element, and the building of a hierarchic power apparatus evoked strong resistance within the Society from members devoted to renewing spiritual life. Many of these members were excluded in 1935. Since Rudolf Steiner's death, the General Anthroposophical Society can no longer claim to be the earthly bearer of the Michaelic movement from the spiritual world. By dissolving the impulse of the Christmas Conference, the Society could fulfill only part of the role intended by Steiner. Anthroposophy should have become a cultural factor, the fount of a new spiritual culture, and help for contemporaries to understand and heal the effect of materialism on their soul. It should take place based on nurturing "the life of the soul, both in the individual and in human society, on the basis of a true knowledge of the spiritual world", as the original statutes stated.

On April 2, 1923, Rudolf Steiner had explained that the movement for social threefolding had failed because Michaelic thought was still too weak. According to him, speaking about the threefolding impulse was an examination of the human soul to see if Michaelic thought was strong enough in even a small number of people.[62] Steiner connected this thinking with the impulse to penetrate the human will with spirituality and to examine the human world of ideas. It has to stimulate social life, he said, so that the forces of decline in human development can be transformed into a rising force. The failure of the Christmas Conference of 1923 can also be associated with this weak Michaelic consciousness. This negative karma has worked, and has produced a terrible outcome, but the new spiritual impulses continue to work. Michael is working everywhere in the world. Since the death of Steiner the impulses of Anthroposophy live in the higher consciousness of humanity.

## 5. Rudolf Steiner's Path of the Cross

A number of anthroposophists from Eastern Europe experienced Rudolf Steiner's life as a Christian path. Andrej Belyi wrote about Rudolf Steiner's path of the cross and the cross of our illnesses he took upon himself.[63] In his book about Steiner and the new mysteries, Sergej Prokofieff wrote of Steiner's four great sacrifices to serve the spiritual world.[64]

---

[62] Rudolf Steiner: *The Cycle of the Year as Breathing Process of the Earth* (1923), Hudson 1988 (CW 223).

[63] Andrej Belyi: *Verwandeln des Lebens*, Basel 1975.

[64] Sergej O. Prokofieff: *Rudolf Steiner and the Founding of the New Mysteries*, London 1994.

In August 1938, Valentin Tomberg, born in St. Petersburg to Estonian parents, held a lecture on Rudolf Steiner's life at an Anthroposophical conference in Rotterdam, Holland.[65] He compared events in Steiner's life to the stations of the Christian medieval path of initiation. Throughout his life Steiner was concerned with problems of others (washing of the feet). He continuously stood between two positions to maintain the middle for the Christ (scourging). He took it upon himself to become a representative of the spiritual world in a materialistic time (crowning with thorns). He became president of the new Society in 1923 by uniting his karma with the members. It was his death (crucifixion). People lost their inner connection to him and were no longer open to new revelations from the spiritual world. Everything was kept in archives and examined (burial). Tomberg said that there is hope for Steiner's resurrection if people erect monuments for him in their inner being (instead of tombstones) to maintain their memory of him. Steiner could fulfill his promise if people have the courage to directly unite with him in the spiritual world.

Steiner paid with his death for the spiritual revolution of inaugurating the new mysteries at the Christmas Conference of 1923. He could not remain on earth because the members did not spiritually awaken and karmic conflicts were not solved. Exactly 33 years after Steiner had joined the Theosophical Society, the General Anthroposophical Society fell apart: the burial was complete.

In conclusion we refer to the words Johanna Countess von Keyserlingk received from Rudolf Steiner out of the spiritual world in the morning of his cremation. They are included in the book *The Birth of a New Agriculture – Koberwitz 1924*, published by her son Adalbert von Keyserlingk:[66]

"My mission has ended."

---

[65] Valentin Tomberg: *Inner Development*, Spring Valley 1983.

[66] Adalbert von Keyserlingk (ed.): *The Birth of a New Agriculture – Koberwitz 1924*, London 2009.

"What I could give to the maturity of man, I have given them."
"I leave because I did not find ears that could perceive the word of the spirit behind the word."
"I leave because I did not find eyes that could see pictures of the spirit behind the pictures of the earth."
"I leave because I did not find people that could realize my will."
"The mysteries remain veiled until I come again."
"I will come again and unveil the mysteries when I can establish an altar in the spiritual worlds, a temple for human souls. Then I come again. Then I will continue to unveil the mysteries."
"Those who have prevented the culture of the heart are guilty of my death."
"If people had reached into the depths through their heart, they would have found the strength to meet the requirements of the current tasks."

In this chapter we have seen how Rudolf Steiner wanted to found a new Anthroposophical Society with a mystery school in which research could be done on the basis of a conscious connection with the spiritual world. The conditions for the development of these new mysteries were not met. These conditions related to an individual path of schooling and the creation of a community in which mutual karma would be harmonized and Anthroposophists would build social temples in their harmonious cooperation. Steiner pointed out three paths to community formation:

1. Religious community formation: this community is formed during worship, because the descending spiritual beings give the congregation a community experience.
2. The Anthroposophical community formation: the cognitive community is formed in the knowledge cult, in which the participants in a conversation about spiritual ideas awaken "on" each other's soul and spirit, ascending with each other

spiritually in a supersensible sphere, where a spiritual being unites them in a spiritual community. This being can also inspire them and give them knowledge.
3. Social community formation: this community arises on the path of the Anthroposophical Social Impulse, which prepares the community life of the next culture.

In the next chapter we will elaborate on how the spiritual world becomes accessible to the awakening consciousness soul in social life, so that people can build mystery centers in social life together. Due to the veiling of the mysteries after Rudolf Steiner's death and the unfinished nature of the School for Spiritual Science, this work can only take place on a limited scale.

CHAPTER IV

# THE SOCIAL WORLD AS MYSTERY CENTER

I. The Long Way towards Summer

Anthroposophy has its own developmental rhythm, as Rudolf Steiner showed in 1923. In its first period (1902-09) Anthroposophy developed within the Theosophical Society. In the language of Theosophy Steiner wrote some fundamental works. The next period (1909-1916) freed Anthroposophy from its theosophical background and Steiner worked steadily in an Esoteric Christian direction. It also unfolded artistically: in the Mystery Dramas, the first Goetheanum and in eurythmy. The third period (1916-1923) saw Anthroposophy step more to the outside in science and social life, pedagogy and therapeutic activities. It came to a conclusion at the Christmas Conference of 1923, after which Steiner began to speak about the karma of the Anthroposophical movement. This set the tone for yet another rhythm.

These three periods can be related to the development of the three forces of soul. The first period concerns the anchoring of the being Anthropo-Sophia in human thinking, the second connects feeling in art, and the third births Anthropo-Sophia in the human will.

Spiritual tradition knows each season of the year to have its own archangel who is also linked to a certain planet. Michael is the archangel of autumn and the regent of the Sun. Gabriel is the archangel of winter and relates to the Moon. Raphael is the archangel of spring and belongs to Mercury, and Uriel is the archangel of summer, working out of the sphere of Saturn. These four archangels represent cosmic streams that we find in the Anthroposophical movement as well. Anthroposophy developed these streams, except for the stream of Uriel.

Anthroposophy's development shows yet another movement, the path through the seasons. Not three periods of seven years are necessary, but four. In 1923, Anthroposophy had not yet matured because it had to pass through one more season, through summer. Because of Steiner's death in 1925, Anthroposophy did not experience summer, the blossoming of its social life.

The influence of Michael, whose name is "Countenance of God" (or literally "who is like God"), is particularly active in the first period of seven years. Michael administered cosmic intelligence before it became earthly. We can spiritualize this intelligence that lives in our thinking and is now materialistically inspired by Ahriman, and give it back to Michael. In 1894, Steiner prepared the spiritualization of intelligence in his book *The Philosophy of Freedom*. This spiritualization can be realized in Anthroposophy to the degree that this philosophy truly comes to life in us. This enlivening takes place in the center of our soul and in art. This is the sphere of Gabriel, "Strength of God". This archangel relates to the forms we create in art and social life. As principle of form, threefolding in the human organism and society is a Gabrielic principle. This is followed by the period of Raphael, "God heals". Healing impulses, so necessary to heal culture from materialism, issue from Raphael. We meet him very concretely in Anthroposophical medicine and therapies, in biologic-dynamic farming, and in curative pedagogy.

The Christmas Conference of 1923 took place at the end of Raphael's period and brought Anthroposophy to Whitsun, celebrated at the end of spring in either May or June. In Whitsun we approach summer. In many ways it is still a festival of the future, because very little spiritual substance is born in our communities that can be carried into the world. This Christmas Conference was an event of Whitsun, inspiring Anthroposophists to go into the world with the Foundation Stone in their hearts to found a new culture. The reality of karma had to awaken, but unfortunately it did not happen, and as a result, Anthroposophy lapsed into a time before Whitsun. Since Rudolf Steiner's death the Anthroposophical movement has hovered between Ascension and Whitsun, as the apostles did. It has faced the question, out of the pain of the failure and concern for the future, how the Whitsun spirit, which should be carried into the world in a fiery way, can be born.

We touch the activity of Uriel, whose name is "Light of God", when spirit is born in us. Uriel represents Saturn, the sphere that relates to our deepest intentions of will, our karmic impulses. In this sphere we unite with others to transform links of destiny or to begin new karma. Uriel has a stern gaze, his gesture admonishing. "He appeals to transform our misdeeds into virtues," said Steiner on October 13, 1923.[67] This takes place in the company of others. New qualities arise when our relationships are rooted in social and

---

67   Rudolf Steiner: *Das Miterleben des Jahreslaufes in vier kosmischen Imaginationen* (1923), Dornach 1989 (CW 229).

religious impulses from the sphere of Uriel. Then the forms inspired by Gabriel can be filled with these impulses.

The new mysteries of the Christmas Conference opened the door to the summer world of Uriel. We experience it very concretely on the path of research begun by Rudolf Steiner and Ita Wegman. She perceived Steiner on the night of the fire; she saw her mistakes and how little help she had so far given. There she stood, in my view, face to face with the Greater Guardian of the Threshold, a spiritual being who stands at the threshold of the spiritual world and shows us our ideal nature in the light of Christ, as Steiner explained.[68] This experience freed her compassion and force of love, and united her with Steiner. Her spirit awakened and something germinated that was later expressed as a question about the new mysteries. Steiner called it the "Percival-question", a question that can arise out of knowing through compassion.

The path of individual initiation leads first of all to the Lesser Guardian of the Threshold, another spiritual being who shows us our true nature of negative and positive qualities.[69] Mutual paths begin by meeting the Greater Guardian, who asks about the other and admonishes us to help and accept him or her. When we truly meet another who we want to associate with out of a social impulse, an aspect of meeting the Christ, showing us the goal of our development as a human being, lights up as well. Then we experience our inadequacies and realize how much work is still to be done. The individual path on the other hand, starting with experiencing our negative aspects, can consequently lead to the Greater Guardian, where the social path begins.

The differences between the individual and the social path of development could be elaborated still further. To me, the individual path seems typically a Western path. It also seems that it is an easier

---

68   Rudolf Steiner: *How to Know Higher Worlds* (1904-1905), Hudson 1994 (CW 10).
69   Ibid.

path for men, or people with a male disposition of soul. It starts with confronting ourselves, which, obviously, is avoided as much as possible, but can always arise in conflicts with others we live and work with. By cultivating self-perception, we can consciously walk a social path on which we develop social forces. The social path is more common for Eastern Europeans, but also for women or female types of soul. Meeting the suffering of others awakens the social impulse to help. We can then notice that our forces are not strong enough, that we have certain inadequacies or bring sacrifices without properly developing our personality. We then have to work on ourselves. Russian folklore contains the motif of meeting the Greater Guardian in many tales. For example, when a peasant on his way meets a person asking for help, and after receiving this help, reveals himself as Christ. Both paths must ultimately be brought together in individual development.

Spirit begins to stream between people and the sun can begin to shine in deep meetings in the sphere of Uriel. The healing Holy Spirit is temporarily active between us, and in such meetings a new consciousness can be born that slumbered in our soul. We can freely associate only in the light and warmth of the summer sun, to found a new spiritual culture. Then the path of Anthroposophy through the seasons is complete in the experience of summer.

The seasons provide a sphere in Anthroposophy for representatives of the four streams of archangels, each with their particular perspective on the social question. In Anthroposophy we can find again the two archangelic axes: The Michael-Raphael axis and the Gabriel-Uriel axis. The Michael group carries the inner fire of thinking, lit by Steiner in *The Philosophy of Freedom*. The Gabriel group represents the arts and the principle of form, the focal point of Marie Steiner von Sivers. The Raphael group has the will to heal, as it lived in Ita Wegman. In the Uriel group live the social and religious impulses where we find Albert Steffen, though he cannot be called a real representative of these Uriel impulses. The Uriel group did not receive a clear profile within Anthroposophy. It is to be found partly in the movement of threefolding, in new forms of social work, in the Christian Community, and outside of the Anthroposophical movement.

These four groups (though obviously not every Anthroposophist has a clear place in them) must unite to help Anthroposophy flow into modern culture. The spiritual situation at the beginning of the 21st century is radically different from the beginning of the 20th century. The social world has become a mystery center where good and evil forces have shown themselves more and more openly in the course of the 20th century. Anthroposophy is the hidden wisdom living within our souls that wants to appear in consciousness. It wants to help us to understand our situation and orient ourselves in the world. Then we can develop a spiritual culture that is able to heal the materialistic world.

This problem we are faced with has four aspects that are sketched in this chapter. First, we need to address the question of how the spiritual world lives in the social world. Then we must ask how we can understand our life as mystery drama, in which meeting others is of increasing importance. Thirdly, we will try to find how we can learn to work with groups and start new social processes. Finally, we ask how we can find a path of development in social life that awakens a social impulse in us.

## 2. The Spiritual World Opens

Since the end of the 19th century the spiritual world is increasingly revealing itself in everyday life, and our inner constitution is changing simultaneously. Social life often confronts us with situations that previously took place in the seclusion of mystery temples or on carefully protected inner paths. We are asked to consciously experience these situations of initiation.

After the First World War, Steiner spoke about the unconscious crossing of the threshold to the spiritual world by humanity, as for example on April 11, 1919.[70] This is part of the epoch of the consciousness soul that began in 1413. This crossing already is taking place after the Archangel Michael purified the sphere surrounding the earth of the so-called "spirits of darkness" (1841-1879). These are fallen angels who hinder us on our path to our higher being. By throwing them to earth he cleared the connection between the sensible and supersensible worlds. Additionally, according to Steiner, since 1899, the end of the Dark Age (Kali Yuga), our constitution began to change. Our life body, or etheric body, is gradually being freed from the physical body so that we can develop new abilities to perceive the spiritual world. The threshold to the spiritual world is becoming transparent. More and more children are born with clairvoyant perceptions, and many people develop such faculties in the course of their life. In the new mysteries we cross the threshold consciously.

Crossing the threshold has significant consequences that were not so perceptible at the beginning of the 20th century. The three naturally connected soul forces of thinking, feeling and willing began to separate. It can be confusing to experience the falling apart of our soul forces because contradictory thoughts, feelings and impulses can arise. Modern humanity must gain control of these forces again and consciously create harmony.

Social life witnesses another development, because in the course of the 19th century the old instinctive threefolding of the social organism was lost. Spiritual, political and economic life was combined in a unitary state and must be consciously separated. On December 14, 1919, Rudolf Steiner said: "The forces of humanity's development, which led

---

[70] Rudolf Steiner, *Vergangenheits- und Zukunftsimpulse im sozialen Geschehen*, Dornach 1980 (CW 190).

people to advance unconsciously, are exhausted and approximately will altogether be gone by the middle of the century."[71] Social forces vanish and make room for egoism.

On November 15, 1919, Rudolf Steiner mentioned that national chauvinism increasingly leads people to split into small groups.[72] On August 6, 1921, he said that, without the social impulse, we would face the war of all against all at the end of the 20th century.[73] And on April 2, 1923: "Whether the descending forces in human development can be transformed again into ascending forces depends first and foremost on introducing the impulse of threefolding."[74]

Without a new, consciously built order the inner world and the social world disintegrate into chaos. As Steiner remarked, the conscious ordering of social life supports the harmonization of the forces of soul as well. Many people experience how unknown forces press into consciousness. Suddenly someone sees a being not perceived by others; sometimes it happens to children and they can experience it as a nature spirit, an angel-like being or a being with evil traits. Someone enters into an inexplicable, violent state or becomes panicky; others perceive aspects of themselves that they do not like to acknowledge. And again, others perceive demonic forces and can be possessed in such a way that we can read it in their faces.

These are unconscious soul forces, or forces from the outside world that did not reach into consciousness previously and now reach us from beyond the threshold of the spiritual world. People react differently with fears, nervousness, depression, and flight into drugs, blind aggression or undefined feelings of discomfort

---

71  Rudolf Steiner: *Michael's Mission* (1919), Forest Row 2016 (CW 194).

72  Rudolf Steiner: *Understanding Society* (1919), Forest Row 2017 (CW 191).

73  Rudolf Steiner: *Menschenwerden, Weltenseele und Weltengeist, Zweiter Teil* (1921), Dornach 1991 (CW 206).

74  Rudolf Steiner: *The Cycle of the Year as Breathing Process of the Earth* (1923), Hudson 1988 (CW 223).

or restlessness. Sometimes neurosis, psychosis or other states in need of treatment arise. By consciously ordering and strengthening their life of soul with the forces of their higher being, many could help themselves. Already on May 30, 1907, Steiner spoke of grave nervous illnesses and epidemics of insanity afflicting whole nations as karmic consequence of materialism.[75] Only spiritual impulses can consciously lead us over the threshold and provide a healing effect, such as on epidemics of nationalism and religious fundamentalism.

The doors to the worlds of light and darkness were opened in the 20th century. According to Rudolf Steiner, this is the beginning of the so-called "Mount of Olives apocalypse" described in the Gospels of Matthew, chapter 24 and Mark, chapter 13. Dark forces are taking hold of people, but the world of good forces is becoming more accessible as well; man stands between the worlds of good and evil. Whether we are conscious or not, the boundary between heaven and hell runs straight through our heart. Modern culture in particular pays much attention to dark forces from the underworld of our subconscious. They enter our soul through the media, and masses of people who are half-asleep are manipulated. Modern art and music, for example, can give a revealing picture of the forces of the collective underworld, the collective subconscious of humanity.

The good forces reveal themselves as well. In contrast to the dark forces, that are not easily chased away when they enter an individual or a group, the good ones respect our freedom. If we do not make them conscious, they go away unnoticed. From 1910 on, Steiner spoke of Christ's Second Coming. He told how the Christ would appear in the sphere of earth's life forces (the etheric sphere), experienced from around 1933 only by a few in the beginning, but leading to more and more people meeting Him in the etheric in the next 2500 years.

---

[75] Rudolf Steiner: *Theosophy of the Rosicrucian* (1907), London 1981 (CW 99).

On October 1, 1911, Steiner described how this might take place.[76] He says that Christ will come to help, comfort and advise people who are at their wit's end, and those who are in deep sympathy with the suffering of others. He also comes to people who search for answers to problems in deep union with others. We can suddenly experience His presence, or even see someone speaking and then just as suddenly disappear. Recognition of the moment is important.

The rise of National Socialism in 1933 darkened the etheric sphere of Christ, but since then many people all over the world experienced help, comfort and healing through Him in existential situations of their lives. Our changed constitution enables us to develop new clairvoyant abilities with which we can form an organ to perceive Him and His activity in the etheric sphere. It is Christ Himself who changes our constitution and makes us clairvoyant so that we can perceive Him. Exercises and strengthening conscience can be of help as well. The near-death experiences represent another aspect of the Second Coming. The experience of Christ in the cycle of the year also develops our powers of perception. Then we connect with the processes of nature in the seasons and experience the celebrations of the year much more consciously.

While the spiritual world gradually opens, the social world becomes the stage of new spiritual experiences. Previously, these took place on a path of initiation, and it is only now that they take place in full life. In everyday life we can meet the experiences described by Rudolf Steiner in How to Know Higher Worlds. This book is about the path of preparing the soul and is helpful to all in our time. What used to be tests as part of initiation in previous times must now be faced in daily life. People already on this path face life more consciously and display self-confidence, courage, steadfastness, self-control and an ability to judge, as well as a presence of mind.

---

[76] Rudolf Steiner: *Esoteric Christianity and the Mission of Christian Rosenkreutz* (1911-1912), London 1984 (CW 130).

People can also experience a splitting of their personality when thinking, feeling and willing separate. This separation also happens on the path of modern initiation, provided by Anthroposophy, when we consciously approach the threshold to the spiritual world. Here we face the Lesser Guardian, who embodies what we have not yet illuminated and transformed with the forces of our higher being. We can meet this guardian in everyday life in various aspects of our double representing our negative and not yet transformed sides. This is also true for the Greater Guardian who represents our pure future image in which Christ points us to our task towards the other.

These experiences become more and more real in the new mysteries because in essence they are new ways to relate consciously to the world of the spirit. It is important that we experience them consciously and learn from them. First and foremost, we must learn to develop our strength of soul with the help of others. It is very important that we make clear judgments and understand what takes place. Then we begin to understand everyday life as a mystery drama where people pass through spiritual development together.

## 3. Daily Life as Mystery Drama

In an interview in 1984 with the German weekly Spiegel, the German artist Joseph Beuys stated: "The mysteries take place at the railway station, not in the Goetheanum." Everyday life has become the place where good and evil forces meet, and no one is excluded from this confrontation. It is often confusing and we do not really know which forces we perceive. For many years we lived in a Cold War drama: one side representing good, the other evil, while both were involved in a devilish armament race. By the time this war ended, a new drama was staged: the Gulf War (1990-91), followed by the threat of Muslim terrorism. Hundreds of millions of souls were faced with a pseudo-choice between good and evil by the mass media and propaganda based on fake news.

Not only on the level of big politics is it difficult to understand and identify the real forces in order to make a moral choice; it is often true for our immediate surroundings as well. Our behavior is usually not transparent; there are conflicts, tensions and misunderstandings. For some people life has turned to chaos, and they notice that they actually do not know what they want or understand what is happening. For many, daily life is disjointed. At the beginning of the 20th century this was hardly the case because life generally still followed the path of traditions and was still regulated by social instincts.

The theosophists whom Steiner connected with at the beginning of his spiritual activity hardly had a need to concretely work with their karma, as most of them were interested in spiritual development only. Personal issues were irrelevant and no one's business, and they were not particularly interested in what takes place between people, either. Rudolf Steiner could not bring them to practical karma exercises, but they were open to dramatic presentations of the soul development of karmically related people, which he created in four mystery dramas between 1910 and 1913. These dramas show the laws of karma and paths of development of soul in artistic form.[77] But the jump from stage to life had to be made. An increasing number of people are initiated by life, and they face unexpected tests for which they could not prepare in seclusion, as was the rule earlier. We must awaken today to each situation and help each other come to judgment. The spiritual world is speaking to us in such tests and unexpected spiritual experiences.

This is also what Steiner addressed in 1922 in answer to young people who had asked him for advice about what they should do in their groups. He said that they should speak about their spiritual

---

77   Rudolf Steiner: *Four Mystery Plays* (1910-1913) (C.W. 14), London 1982 (CW 14).

experiences. When they objected and told him that they did not yet have any spiritual experience to talk about, he replied that they have spiritual experiences daily, but have just let them go unnoticed. What does this mean? Everyone can briefly experience his spirit awakening. An assumption, an idea, a question or an insight arises, or the soul takes hold of an ideal. Our conscience speaks, or we sense a connection to a spiritual being, or we wake up with a meaningful image. Every person has these experiences when open to them.

We begin to perceive spiritually what is taking place in the world around us, in our lives or in our groups. This can happen spontaneously, but this may have been prepared by doing transformative work with our soul and by creating a connection with our higher being. By doing exercises we can develop our spiritual organs of perception (chakras) and receive imaginations, inspirations and intuitions in our higher consciousness. We can also become sensitive to how our angel accompanies us and calls up certain moments of karma and to the activity of Christ in our life.

Daily life continuously provides us with spiritual experiences that lead us to cross the threshold to the spiritual world. They can also be the result of the use of drugs, crises, psychic shock, illness, unemployment, loneliness and death, or creative moments and religious experiences. Steiner's mystery dramas can serve as examples. In them the spiritual teacher Benedictus is able to interpret what the others experience, but we have to find our own path among the opposing forces in the labyrinth of life. We must interpret our spiritual experiences in conversations, learn to concretely understand the processes of development of soul and spirit and discover how we can make the entanglements of life transparent.

Anthroposophical literature describes the processes concerning our development of soul (in their male and female variations) that lead to the birth of the human spirit. Many authors since Rudolf Steiner have written with increasing clarity about the development of soul and its deviations. The awakening of the spirit in human biography is a new terrain that is gradually being discovered. Our spirit can awaken when we make an important decision, when we better understand our life tasks, when we are tested by suffering and still continue, when we take initiative or social impulses. Our awakening higher Self will guide our soul forces, take control of the forces of our double and integrate the male and the female aspects of our soul. It has the key to understand the mystery that takes place in daily life.

The social world has become a mystery center. We are always surrounded by spiritual beings, and we can perceive that. Their quality is determined by us. People and groups with negative thoughts, feelings and actions attract negative spiritual beings and nourish them with their negativity. These beings do not leave, and may force us to give them more nourishment. This is the phenomenon of the double. In contrast to them, individuals with a positive radiance and groups cooperating in a positive spirit are surrounded by friendly spiritual beings, who can be invited to support and inspire them.

For this reason it is so important for all spiritual groups to cultivate a conscious social life. Otherwise they will fall victim to their group doubles. In the present conditions of our consciousness this is rather normal, but we have to know how to purify and heal the etheric and astral space that has been polluted by group doubles, and to resolve the conflicts that arise between people. In Anthroposophical circles this was in the past a neglected area of attention.

In the already mentioned lectures of February 27 and March 3, 1923, on Anthroposophical community building, Rudolf Steiner spoke of the increasing need to awaken "on" the other and of the necessity to become someone for the other to awaken "on". The individual path becomes more difficult to the degree that we end up in a dead-end road with our personality, our ego. We seek to meet others, but due to our unsocial drives it becomes increasingly more difficult.

Awakening "on" and "in" the other is a gradual process that can take place in meetings. Steiner described how someone speaks and others awaken "on" their words or in the ensuing conversation. Depending on the degree to which the spoken word is suffused by the forces of heart, awakening brings us from the sphere of ideas to the world of immediate experiences. This is also true for awakening "on" another person's impulses. We must experience them before we can accept them consciously. In order to come to a true experience, we must enliven ideas and impulses in our feeling.

We can only arrive at a deeper awakening once we well connected with our body and soul. In the first 21 years of life we acquire the use of our threefold body (physical, etheric and astral). Then follows the development of soul, which includes our personality and unsocial drives that provide our place in the world. Each person develops a particular one-sidedness, until a point of arresting is reached. For some this already happens early in their development, and large parts of the soul remain idle and not yet conscious. Others close off in their personality and begin to feel lonely. In the middle of life, around the 35th year, a new source of strength can become active in the soul. This strength comes from our higher being making room in the soul for the individual spirit to be born around the 40th year. According to Rudolf Steiner, the spirit has a balancing and integrating effect on the male and female aspects of the human soul.[78]

Only since the mystery of Golgotha the spirit can be born in us. The spirit used to act from the outside, but now it can work from the inside out and awaken as individual spirit. We are renewed in spiritual activity by a constant broadening of consciousness, and experience freedom in this process. The apostle Paul was the first to indicate this new person. The old human being within is bound to

---

78  Rudolf Steiner: "The Separation of the Sexes", in *Cosmic Memory* (1904-1908), New York 1990 (CW 11).

threefold physicality. He is the product of our past. The new human being is the spirit-child in the lap of the soul. He is the human being coming from the future. In order to give birth to and unite with this child and the forces of childhood within, we must die and let go of the old human being within (pass through an inner Golgotha). Christ's power of resurrection effects this transformation from old to new, from bound to free.

Once self-consciousness stabilizes in the middle of life we can pass through this process more consciously. But first of all consciousness must be expanded, which takes place when we awaken "on" the other. The awakening of our individual spirit also awakens social forces. Now we can consciously take the other into ourselves and ask the appropriate awakening questions in conversation. The other can then awaken "in" us. To be social and open to the other we must form our soul space. That is, develop our personality.

We can also distinguish between an Anthroposophy that we receive from outside, for example from Rudolf Steiner and an Anthroposophy that streams from us into the world. In that case we should not treat what Steiner said as the truth, but as information that we have to check before it can become our knowledge. We can do this by using our sound judgment, our sense of truth. Only then it can become our personal Anthroposophy, the fruit of our own spiritual activity. This is the application of Steiner's book *The Philosophy of Freedom*. It shows the way to the intuitive thinking that can overcome dogmatism.

The events of the mystery drama of daily life relate to our processes of soul, to the transformation from old to new. Each moment can give us new insights that we owe to others. Corresponding to the level of self-consciousness, our inadequacies and ego-armor can become transparent to us. They often play a large role in conflicts. We get annoyed with negative aspects of ourselves that we project on others, and do not want to see in ourselves. These aspects constitute our double that is found in the spaces of our threefold bodies not yet filled with our consciousness and often shows up in interhuman relationships. Occasional events of friction teach us to deal with our conflicts; they can awaken us and create order in our own house. Each conflict provides a possibility of inner development.

A modern development of soul leads us through conflicts with others and confrontations with our inadequacies. Through a process of purification new spiritual forces can arise out of these imperfections. It belongs to the tasks of our time to understand and accept the depths and dark sides of our soul. We have to allow our egoism in order to recognize our responsibility towards others in dealing with it. Then we can be consciously social. We must also learn to consciously manage the forces of the unconscious, otherwise their activity remains veiled. The further we develop spiritually, the deeper we must descend into our underworld to handle these forces in a moral way and in the light of consciousness.

New aspects of daily life can be illuminated in meeting others, also in the sphere of karma; it provides extraordinary opportunities to clarify issues. When we speak about our experiences to others an event can become transparent and the other can help us live into the situation. Gradually we clarify increasing areas of daily life and can face them with greater inner strength. Speaking to others about our life can help to reveal the meaning of certain events. We can order our life and clear the way for new phases where we act more consciously. We can also discover something of the karma that weaves between us, order our relationships, and learn to cooperate and create possibilities for new, self-chosen connections. In real meetings we learn to ask much deeper questions. My karma can be revealed in a question put to me; questions I ask the other can express his or her karma. My life can change when I pay attention to deep questions from someone I feel connected to. These questions do not come by chance, but appear only when we deeply connect.

Real meetings have a certain pattern that usually arises only in the course of a number of meetings:
1. Each meeting begins with a preparation. We adjust to the other; we inwardly make room, accept him or her into ourselves as they appear outwardly, and ask a question.
2. Then we listen with reverence and tolerance to what the other has to say. The other fills our consciousness and leaves a picture of his or her circumstances.
3. We can inwardly process this picture, perceive the spiritual reality, and receive a first idea of the karma in his or her circumstance or between us. We can also deepen this impression with karma exercises (as found in Steiner's lecture of May 9, 1924, in the book *Karmic Relationships*).[79]
4. In the next step we can return what we received and inwardly processed, or let it be followed by mutual activity. We can also express in words what we have heard and understood so that the other can perceive it as correct or incorrect. Then we can act in freedom out of the circumstance of the meeting, thus creating new karma.

To the degree that we can submit to the other, a deep meeting has the character of a sacrament; it becomes a cultic act as we find it in liturgy. In such encounters etheric connections are created with others. In his book on the social sacraments, Dieter Brüll pointed to the inner connection of the individual elements of this consciously experienced conversation and the four parts of liturgy:[80]
1. A purification in which egoistic drives are silenced.
2. The sacrifice of self-consciousness can fill me with the other.
3. Taking into ourselves what lives in the other is transformation.
4. What I give back in word or deed is communion.

---

79  Rudolf Steiner: *Karmic Relationships*, Vol. 2 (1924), London 1975 (CW 236).

80  Dieter Brüll: *Creating Social Sacraments*, AWSNA Research Institute for Waldorf Education, Wilton 2010.

Meetings can be mutual when we listen to what each has to say, or the meeting is one-sided if only the other wants to relate and clarify. The latter is also true for new forms of psychosocial work, when people want to create a picture of their biography or are in need of therapeutic accompaniment. In biographical conversations we can tell the story of our life, order events, differentiate phases of life, bring the life of soul to consciousness and discover meaning in events or things we cannot or do not want to understand We can also learn to perceive what is coming to us from the future. In this way we can find new strength to go on. The other helps by creating a picture of our life and returning it to us.

We can help others in the sense of the social impulse through conversation so that their spirit awakens and they realize something new. It provides new strength to order their relationships differently. Much more is asked of us if we want to accompany someone therapeutically. To a certain degree we must substitute the ego-function of the other. In both instances one-sidedness can be overcome by shared conversation and increased understanding of ourselves through the other: this includes inadequacies and shortcomings as well as real possibilities.

In the moving pendulum of the archetypal phenomenon of communication we cross the threshold to the spiritual world, together with the other person, in every gesture of falling asleep and waking up. When we learn to master these movements consciously in conversation and hold on to what we heard in awakening, the meeting can become an inexhaustible fount of spiritual experiences and insights.

When two or more people are together in the name of Christ, He will be in their midst. Here the community of the future arises, when we gather in deep morality and a shared inner experience in the name of Christ. The last chapter will explain this kind of community building, with the help of the Social Impulse of Anthroposophy, in more detail.

People can be supportive and have a healing effect on each other in meetings and social relationships based on a social impulse. They can help each other in their karma, the consequences of past actions, and a community can help carry the individual karma. If we hold the others in our thoughts, pray for them, create an image of them and of what they carry in their soul as impulse of will, we then help them when they no longer know what they really want. We then hold on to what we perceived of the other's life task in the meeting. When we are companions in each other's destinies, the mystery drama of everyday life acquires a very different character. Life becomes more transparent, and we can play a more self-conscious role with the help we receive from others.

New qualities of helping each other can arise in social relationships, resulting in increased self-awareness and consciousness, bringing each other to spiritual experiences. It could be the spiritual purpose of modern partnerships in which two people support each other in their growth process. Celtic Christianity knew of a social relationship called "soul friendship". A monk had a nun as a soul sister and vice versa. They helped each other on their way to Christ. In modern language we would say that they lovingly mirrored each other and gave each other feedback. The later Middle Ages show this phenomenon again in the friendships of Saint Francis and Saint Clara of Assisi, Abaelard and Heloise, the troubadour and his lady, the poet and his muse and many others. Today these relationships become increasingly important to soul development and for a living connection with the spiritual world. They show us small mystery centers created by two human beings and point to entirely new forms of cooperation that can also include more than two persons.

## 4. Learning to Cooperate

In the society Rudolf Steiner founded in 1923 we cannot be Anthroposophists unto ourselves. We must cooperate, as we can only progress in social life by associations with others. In conversations and meetings with others new possibilities appear that did not exist before. Steiner wanted the co-authorship of the book on Anthroposophical medicine with Ita Wegman. They discussed the topics together, and then Wegman wrote the first version that was worked through by Steiner. He wanted the new medicine to pass through her soul and be formulated in her brain, as it was not yet disfigured by intellectualism. Here we can see the new mysteries in action: two people (or more) initiate each other in a certain area of spiritual experience. The spiritual perception of one person sounds forth in the soul of the other and leads to new insights.

Their cooperation can be an example for other Anthroposophists who go into the world to work spiritually. At the closing of the Christmas Conference of 1923 Rudolf Steiner indicated that we need to place the Foundation Stone in our heart so we can, in cooperation with others, build our spiritual work in the world on it. A spiritual Goetheanum can be built anywhere; groups can build future spiritual-social mystery temples wherever they are.

It is by no means easy to found such mystery centers. Ideas and impulses collide wherever people come together. Some people live very strongly in the world of ideas but find it difficult to come to deeds out of their ideas. Meetings with others are necessary to bring ideas into the sphere of experience and of feeling, and then they can descend to the will and lead to practical acts. All is general in the sphere of ideas, but we have to make them our own and unite with them in our hearts so that they can become fruitful in practice. Others are more practical and simply go ahead with their impulses of will. In order to share these impulses, they must be brought into conversation to unite them with feeling, so they can be expressed in words and understood by everyone. A continuous movement that passes through the sphere of feeling, where we connect with others, can arise between ideas and impulses.

This sphere of feeling is not free of sympathies and antipathies, and we always find conflicts that, of course, are also present in conflicting ideas and impulses. But the life of feeling provides the possibility of transforming sympathies and antipathies into loving interest. However, this requires much self-consciousness. An atmosphere filled with heart forces can arise in a group of people when its members find the strength to try and understand each other, mutually adjust ideas or find a common impulse. Groups do not last long without this sphere. Trust can then arise and people can get to know each other in their peculiarities. It is of utmost importance that we get to know and understand the male and female qualities in ourselves and the corresponding peculiarities in each other's soul, because it is the foundation of any human cooperation.

Some groups concentrate in particular on developing ideas, others on realizing certain impulses. These study or initiative groups cannot exist if communication in meetings is not cultivated. A third kind of group is concerned with just that: communication. It is the social group where people gather to get to know each other, right down to their destiny. By these meetings we gradually come to recognize our own karma and that of others. We get to know people with very different intentions of will and discover what speaks in the image of the other, how they (and ourselves) are imprisoned by old karma, and how they create a new future. We can learn to look through the double and see the actual human being they really want to be. If we are awake, we can also perceive aspects of our own double.

What we thus experience provides new possibilities to look back and learn from our past. It also helps us to understand others and associate, particularly if they speak about their life and personal development. We now begin to understand why others are the way they are and what lives in them.

We enter the sphere of rights when we live or work with others and strive to ascertain our relationship to them. Rights do not concern an individual and his moral intentions but the mutual protection of human beings. The sphere of rights is not obvious. It only exists when we are conscious of and perceive each other as equals, in all our peculiarities. Only with this conscious perception can we develop a sense of righteousness and a consciousness of rights and duties. This is why we must cultivate human interaction. Associations with many people involved often have no time to do just this. We often see others primarily in their expertise, abilities or negative aspects, but not their purely human qualities that only appear in meeting them. In the sphere of rights we experience crossing the threshold when we temporarily give up our ego-position to take the position of the other. Many do not want to experience this moment of death, or give up power over the situation.

If the sphere of rights is not rooted in a consciousness of people's fundamental equality it will then fall victim to the power of experts and interest groups. This will clearly show when it comes to decisions. Are all participants equal partners or is the decision made by someone with expertise or interests? In these cases, forces from the sphere of culture (expertise, abilities, ideas) or economy (interests, egoism, money) can break into the sphere of law. We are usually not clear about it, but a feeling of discomfort as well as an unconscious tendency to undermine what was thus decided arises out of a violated sense of rights.

Where we work together with others we can learn to perceive this and a consciousness of rights and duties can awaken. We need social threefolding to protect this sphere. It does not represent an effective force as idea alone. It only reveals its relevance when it is linked to experiences and concrete possibilities. Steiner only called attention to social threefolding to answer questions of life perceived in that particular moment and within the possibilities of the situation at the time. Presently we can gather very important experiences in the field of social threefolding in meso social life and in concrete cultural and economic initiatives. Can we communicate well in these initiatives and do we create the sphere where we are equals? Can we activate this sphere of rights to make proper arrangements? In general, on the macro level of society we can help to awaken a consciousness of rights and influence political decisions. What is fundamental is learning to cooperate and recognizing that the protection of others is the actual source of law.

We need not yet be social (or morally perfect) to work in a threefold social structure that includes a sphere of rights. To become social is a possibility on our path of individual development. No one can force us to be social. The task of social threefolding is to provide the possibility of relationships to be social. It obviously can support us to become social and develop social impulses, but threefolding does not make particular demands. It leaves us free to fill it with content. With a sphere of rights threefolding provides the possibility of a sphere that is free of rulership, and experience each other as equals when making decisions. Equality as principle does not exist in spiritual and economic life. They are the realms of freedom (spiritual life) and brotherhood (economic life) respectively.

In a life or work community, rules do not have a perfect form. They arise in the course of time and according to the developing consciousness of rights. The social process creates its own social forms: consultations, appointments, rules, procedures and laws. In the beginning these are flexible, then harden as they are finally formalized. Now the social process runs in a bureaucratic routine. A consciousness of rights must be activated again when flexibility disappears. To create social forms, that is, bring people's attitudes to expression and maintain a consciousness of rights, is a social art that must be learned. It is a "regal art", as Rudolf Steiner remarked on January 2, 1906.[81]

At first we will often tend to dictate rules out of thinking or objective interests, until we discover that we cannot live with an agreement and will want to abolish it again. But the starting point must be whether the other, for whom the rule was created, can live with it and is protected by it from my unsocial tendencies. My social behavior towards another person as it is expressed in a certain form is the issue. This form, a rule prohibiting me from something for example, makes me face a fact. In coming up against it, I wake up in my inability to adhere to it, and then I can educate myself. Rules and laws given from above used to educate us. Now they must come from within, and we have to educate ourselves in social life.

Something that questions all future juristic thinking appears in our time. It is the voice of conscience replacing the stream of law. Conscience arose in the first centuries before Christ as an organ to perceive Him. It is the voice of Christ in us, and therefore is the voice of the other in us. If we behave badly with each other in the social process, we not only violate rules but will also hear the voice of conscience. Here we can see Uriel's admonishing gesture. On October 12, 1923, Rudolf Steiner said that Uriel activates historic conscience.[82] An inner law arises, rendering outer law and the legal sphere superfluous in the future.

In social processes we can discover that our social attitude is unsatisfactory, and these inadequacies can play a role as aspects of doubles. Social processes are a continuous practice of confronting ourselves and opportunities to awaken. Because we cannot force others to be social, we can only make that decision for ourselves.

---

[81] Rudolf Steiner, *The Temple Legend* (1904-1914), London 1985 (CW 93).

[82] Rudolf Steiner: *Das Miterleben des Jahreslaufes in vier kosmischen Imaginationen* (1923), Dornach 1989 (CW 229).

Two complementary paths exist: inner and outer law. We can make rules to remind others of their unsocial behavior and be reminded ourselves (via a guardian of rules and agreements), but we would never be able to tie down every aspect of a double with these rules and agreements. It is therefore a matter of how long others want and can tolerate us, and vice versa.

The path of inner law is much more difficult because then we must carry each other in our inabilities, and want to see the inabilities of others as our own. It is the future path of perceiving good intentions in the other, of forgiving and carrying the inability and deeds of others. On this path we learn to accept the other's incompleteness as a purely human trait out of a consciousness of how difficult it is to change something in ourselves. Maybe we even learn to be with people we actually do not like.

We can also discover how much we change in social processes because we are on our way together and learn to better understand each other. We can awaken "on" each other and come to consciousness of our inabilities in social life. Sometimes we have moments of an awakening consciousness in seminars, or through practicing social exercises. These exercises do not make us social, but they confront us with ourselves. This, of course, can only happen in an atmosphere of freedom. We cannot set out to adjust someone's behavior and social abilities. In social life we act responsibly towards others and no one should manipulate us. Social life is the true school for developing social behavior from the inside out, in the form of a new social attitude, for example.

By creating an area of rights, in addition to spiritual and economic aspects of life, wherever we associate, our work or living together receives a heart where everything flows together and where we can then make common decisions. However, it is not easy to be continuously conscious of which question belongs to the sphere of rights; that is, which question concerns all. But only this consciousness maintains a threefold whole.

Forces from the past are still active in the present. The principles of power and hierarchy, purposeful in the past and even up to the beginning of the 20th century, destroy all social processes today. They do not allow true meetings or the development of a free consciousness of rights. These principles of power and hierarchy are also present in anthroposophical institutions, and can only be overcome by social threefolding. To the degree that this can take place, inter-human life with its sphere of rights is humanized. It is not by chance that Rudolf Steiner spoke in particular of the right to self-determination of free individualities when Woodrow Wilson spoke of the right of self-determination of nations in 1917. It concerns the free human being; freed in political life from every authority, hierarchy, and slavery in work conditions. It was the impulse of democratization in the 1960s that slowly found its way into Anthroposophical institutions, but still is not solidly established everywhere.

Democratic conditions of rights do not allow being inconsiderate of others within an organization. Mandates should be given to nominated, skilled people, and for a limited time by an assembly of the decision-making group. It gives people the right to appear aristocratic or republican within their mandates, but they are accountable and return their mandate when the time is up. The mandate is based on the group's trust in a particular individual. This quality of trust is the foundation of a new social order that must replace social life based on distrust and control.

Completely new possibilities arise when people learn to cooperate. The new mysteries are then enacted on a certain level. The example of Rudolf Steiner and Ita Wegman shows how we can lead each other to new spiritual experiences in meetings and forms of cooperation created on the basis of equality. This is the ultimate reason why we should create the appropriate social forms with so much care. They make spiritual experiences possible where old forms prevent them.

When we perform the "knowledge cult", new possibilities can also open in group conversations that appear in a conversation between two persons who consciously apply the social archetypal phenomenon. When we are willing to listen to each other it can happen that, rather unexpectedly, certain intuitions, insights and experiences that live in several people but were not clear before are expressed. It can be a conversation where the participants want to express experiences in words, try to solve a certain problem or formulate insights more meditatively. I have experienced several times that connections from heart to heart suddenly arose among participants and how this etheric stream brought light and warmth to the group. The spirit weaves between people in Whitsun moments like this.

What people make possible for each other in this way can be compared to an initiation, in a certain sense, of course. We enter the spiritual world through each other by reacting to shared experiences, perceptions and ideas, and lasting human connections arise. Certain conditions must be fulfilled in order to experience these new mysteries, on the modest level that is open to us non-initiates:

- There is a concrete question or topic on which to unite in thinking, feeling and willing.
- The participants have an objective ability to judge and understand the other from the inside out. This requires a developed consciousness soul.
- Partnership is essential to the group; no authority based on expertise or status.
- We speak out of our own experience and refrain from referring to someone else's ideas.
- Everyone thinks the thoughts of others and continues them.

- The participants can ask spiritual beings to inspire them, be aware of their presence, and be open to their possible inspirations.
- To a certain degree the karma within this group must be ordered through getting to know each other and finding a basis for cooperation.

Often a person then says what several people could have said in that moment. In these groups we can realize something new, obviously with all its limitations and possibilities of illusion. Of course, the reality of the present is that we are still hardly able to cooperate. It is already a difficult task to develop and purify our soul; for many the social impulse still lies far away.

There are nevertheless people who discover these new possibilities, and step by step they prepare a new culture. They draw their strength from each other and their associations can be vessels into which spiritual beings can descend to act through individuals. On November 23, 1905, Steiner spoke about what we now can gradually discover, which is that people working in brotherhoods are magicians because they draw higher beings into their circle.[83] The deceased ones, angels and other spiritual beings can act in social life through groups. Steiner once said that new revelations from the spiritual world would in future be given only to these communities of people. His cooperation with Marie Steiner, Edith Maryon and Ita Wegman was the first example of this new kind of revelation. Groups of cooperating people can then become mystery centers where the spirit can work in a healing way and the spiritual world can inspire people to renew culture.

Also modern science has discovered that cooperation can be a source of inspiration. Groups of researchers and think tanks have been formed for all kinds of projects. A good example is the Manhattan project in America, where the first nuclear weapons

---

83  Rudolf Steiner: *Die Welträtsel und die Anthroposophie* (1905- 1906), Dornach 1983 (CW 54).

were manufactured. In their "knowledge cult" the members of the project group were united by a demonic being into a community that received inspirations from the spirits of darkness. Time pressure and competition for research funds may create an atmosphere where the moral and spiritual consciousness of the researchers can be darkened. In that condition they are open to inspirations for new weapons and technologies, such as most recently 5G, the new generation of wireless communication.

Personal ambition, power, abstract scientific thinking, overload and stress further heighten receptivity to these inspirations. Thus the dark picture of the new mysteries appears in science as an anti-Whitsun. Also organizations outside the area of science know the value of self-organizing synergetic teams, in which ideas from the spiritual world can be received.

Researchers inspired by Anthroposophy attempt to work in various institutes and research groups in the sense of the new mysteries and to show the alternative of a new spiritual science. A science that clearly presents how the living Christ is active in human development, in the history of mankind, in healing processes, in nature as well as in human society. It was the task of the School for Spiritual Science to work with spiritual research, but after Steiner's death it was not clear how the School should be led, because he did not name a successor. Spiritual research based on the "knowledge cult" is still modest, but it is growing.

Nowadays there are many people who can perceive spiritual beings. This is not enough to create a new culture. They must cooperate. Also, people who do not have spiritual perceptions can form circles and research groups to work together. This requires that people associate in friendship and learn to cooperate. Individuals must walk a path of development together to build community and develop organs to perceive the spiritual world in social life.

# 5. The Path of Social Development

Anthroposophists are familiar with the path of schooling presented by Rudolf Steiner in *How to Know Higher Worlds*. He recommends a path leading to the development of soul forces and self-education. At a later stage we learn to form the organs to perceive the spiritual world. Step by step this path leads to initiation where organs of perception are opened that we need to communicate with the spiritual world. It can then present us with gifts of certain experiences and perceptions. However, in the beginning we should not imagine it to be too grandiose, though. It begins with sensitized perception and increased observance.

A new person grows within on this individual path of initiation and development. Our spirit awakens. Steiner described the different experiences we will have in this process. He says that at different stages, we can consciously meet the two Guardians of the Threshold. Since the latter half of the 19th century humanity has unconsciously crossed over the threshold to the spiritual world. We have unconscious experiences in daily life that also appear on the path of schooling, where they are experienced consciously. It is important that we acquire this consciousness in our daily lives, and Anthroposophy offers this help by consciously guiding us to the threshold of the spiritual world. The lessons of the first class of the School for Spiritual Science support this process.

People on their own inner path do not yet create a new culture; it happens only when we learn to work with others. Cooperation faces us with entirely new problems; we gain new spiritual experiences and new insights. New ways of collaborative research open up to complement the individual path of spiritual research. These new ways, of course, do not substitute for the individual path. We have to manage the forces of soul and develop our personality when we work with others in order to arrive at spiritual knowledge on common paths of research.

We see the essence of these paths of research when we observe Rudolf Steiner and Ita Wegman's cooperation that began in 1923 and led to the inauguration of the new mysteries. In Torquay, August 1924, Steiner spoke with gratitude about this cooperation in the lectures *True and False Paths of Spiritual Investigation*.[84] He pointed to the great importance of this path of research next to the individual path described in *How to Know Higher Worlds*. On this new path we can discover the secrets of the outer world based on modern, objective consciousness and a deep inner (and karmic) connection.

On this path, prepared by Rosicrucians in the late Middle Ages, it is essential to relate perceptions, spiritual experiences and insights while researching the outer world. Steiner indicated in *True and False Paths of Spiritual Investigation* that we lose these experiences if we do not share them in conversation. They must pass through the soul of the other and return to us. Steiner and Wegman anticipated and prepared what we can further develop in all areas of researching natural phenomena.

On August 16, 1920, in the lecture *Forming Social Judgment*, Steiner spoke about the differences between forming a judgment in spiritual, political and economic life.[85] Accordingly, a new social order must be built on the basis of these judgments as they lead to true knowledge in the three spheres of social life. Two people can fructify each other and form a judgment about spiritual questions in spiritual life, as shown by the German poets Goethe and Schiller, for example. Mature people face each other in political life. Judgment of rights and duties arises in reciprocal actions that correspond to

---

84   Rudolf Steiner: *True and False Paths in Spiritual Investigation* (1924), London 1985 (CW 243).

85   Rudolf Steiner and Roman Boos: "Die Bildung eines sozialen Urteils" in *Gegenwart*, Nr. 7-9 (1950).

our sense of rights. We can judge in economic life only out of cooperation when each person has practical economic experiences.

We must learn to cooperate in these different ways of judging. According to Steiner, judgment in economic life should take place in associations where consumers, distributors and producers regulate production, circulation and consumption of goods. It is also possible that in the realm of spiritual life more than two people can cooperate. This can lead to common work in founding a school, for example. New karma arises out of this. It is not necessary that people already know each other from past lives.

Rudolf Steiner left it to the groups of cooperating Anthroposophists to further elucidate the paths of research and cognition. This is difficult without the direct help of an initiate, as many conflicts have revealed our inability. Nevertheless, groups that manage to cooperate break through traditional opinions to develop a new Anthroposophy through creative processes. For example a group of teachers who try to understand the symptoms of the times and change the curriculum so that the teaching is geared more towards the problems of the children. Or when a group of physicians and therapists, trying to understand an aspect of disease, develop a new medicine or therapy; when farmers solve problems in agriculture, or psychologists and curative pedagogues discuss how they can help a child with special psychic problems; and when members of a research institute do research together. They all may experience the help of spiritual beings.

This experience of the new mysteries can happen in short inspired moments that provide answers to practical questions, as is also possible in a child or patient consultation. When teachers or therapists share their perceptions, this can sometimes lead to true insight that they create together. Also two persons who discuss a common problem may experience this, for example a couple discussing the solution of an educational problem. In performing the "knowledge cult "such a group might become a temporary mystery center in which spiritual beings give their inspirations.

The discussions in these groups begin with a more or less conscious experience of the Greater Guardian. We feel asked to help another person or accomplish a certain task in the world. There's a problem on the table that can be discussed or investigated in various ways. In a next step, the aspects of the problem will be visualized. The method of Goethean phenomenology (the open-minded observation of phenomena and the discovery of what they have to say to us) can be helpful here. This is the phase of image creation. When the most important points have become visible, the group can proceed to the formation of a judgment. This can then finally lead to a solution. Spiritual beings can be inspiring. Whether the insight gained is true and whether the solution found is valuable, remains to be seen.

When we compare these phases of the "knowledge cult" with the stages of the religious cult the following picture emerges:
1. Posing the problem corresponds to the prelude.
2. To hold back one's own interpretations when forming an objective image is the offering.
3. Transforming one's own prejudices in the formation of judgment is transformation.
4. The union with the spiritual world in finding the solution is communion.

Inspirations of spiritual beings cannot be enforced. They come as an act of 'grace' when the group is ready. There must also be people in the group who can receive them. When a community in the sense of the Social Impulse of Anthroposophy has arisen in the group, these inspirations take place in a "social etheric" temple.

Concrete cooperation in the "knowledge cult" does not lead to an initiation as Steiner described in *How to Know Higher Worlds*.

We have to speak of a different initiation when people initiate each other. In conversation and cooperation people share certain spiritual experiences as gifts. What one says resounds in the soul of the other and leads to new experiences and ideas. The participants in conversation fructify each other. Each person relates to and shares certain aspects of the spiritual world, thus providing others access to it and allowing the group to become a vessel into which it can speak.

By consciously applying the archetypal phenomenon of communication in dialogues and by practicing the "knowledge cult" in group conversations, the social sphere becomes an organ where we can perceive the spiritual world. Some of the conditions for this were described in this chapter. We must follow an individual path of development that allows our consciousness soul to mature, consciously applying the archetypal phenomenon of communication, developing the art of conversation, and learning to cooperate through conflict. We have to be willing to perceive and mirror each other in a loving way and observe and discuss the social process as well. Meditating the mantras from the class lessons can help to become familiar with inspirations from spiritual beings.

The social path of development offers us a very different picture of each other. We begin to perceive the others as our door to the spiritual world. We must be able to hold ourselves back in order to give the other person enough space in the social process. John the Baptist, whose motto "He has to grow, I diminish," reminds us of this when pointing to the Christ. Applied to social life, we must become smaller so that the other can grow. St. John's festival is celebrated on June 24, the beginning of summer, and the starting point of the path of the Whitsun community (individuals going into the world) that leads to Michael's festival on September 29. We can experience the Baptist inspiring communities of people on a social path who build islands of a new culture carried by the spirit.

This modesty, for the sake of development of another, was particularly perceptible in the life of Rudolf Steiner. He constantly held back his intentions and came to deeds only out of requests by others who came to him. He gave himself completely over to them. He listened and they came to themselves; he perceived them and they awakened in him. They felt supported, saw their life's task and felt reborn as human beings, strengthened and healed in their being. He inspired them to spiritual experiences. He posed a few questions and listened, and then he was able to lead the other through his soul into the spiritual world and give them the gift of a small initiation. In this conversation they were connected with their higher being.

If we live out of social impulses and form a community in cooperation, then cultivating the forces of the heart must be daily work. The Foundation Stone Meditation that Steiner gave at the Christmas Conference places a foundation for spiritual work in our heart and builds up its forces. In How to Know Higher Worlds, Steiner had already pointed to the cultivation of heart forces, when he described the six subsidiary exercises on the individual path of initiation. These exercises strengthen the soul so that our higher nature learns to control the soul forces of thinking, feeling and willing. These are exercises to master thinking and action, to develop patience and endurance, tolerance and positivity, impartiality and equanimity.

When we exercise these virtues, peace enters our heart and we can perceive what takes place in the souls of others. The heart then becomes an organ of perception. Cooperation with others is improved when we follow these exercises. They belong to the social path of development as well and can be practiced in every conversation. They add to the art of conversation and remind us to be conscious of what is appropriate in relationships. For example: respecting the other, refraining from criticizing without being asked, allowing the other to finish speaking, speaking no longer than necessary, sticking to a topic and appointed time, avoiding use of the emotions of others, and so forth.

This cooperation also demands that we perceive the world with clear consciousness to form judgments. Steiner appeals to the ability of clear thought and the development of our ability to judge. The path he indicates is shown in *The Philosophy of Freedom*. We can read it like a book of exercises by following the course of the text and continuously asking whether we understand the train of thought. When we stop at a place we do not understand and concentrate on the text, forces are set free that help us to understand the world and ourselves and we can act out of insight. It is not important how fast we proceed or how long we need to read it. It helps to experience our thoughts in the heart, to judge rightly and let the moral intentions of our heart become active in our deeds.

The paths of cognition known to the old mysteries, the path to the inner world (leading to experiences and knowledge of the inner world and to self-knowledge) and the path to the outer world (leading to knowledge of the outer world) are combined in Anthroposophy. The Middle Ages knew these two paths as mystical and chymical paths. In our time we also have the path of social development, the path to the other human being.

The modern paths of researching the inner and the outer world are based on the union of the male forces of thinking and willing. In the center of our soul, in feeling, our female qualities of soul live that unite us with the world and with others. Thinking and willing can develop through meditation and concentration, but this is not true for feeling. It has its own path of development in the transformation of the heart forces. This path is the social path of development described above, when our heart leads the life of feeling and shows its highest force in love; it is the path of the social impulse that leads to community building and mutual research.

The being of Sophia, incorporated in Mary, was present amidst Christ's pupils at the first Whitsun festival. From the 20th century on she is present among people as Anthropo-Sophia to open the path to the new mysteries via the new Whitsun experience of the Christmas Conference of 1923. The male forces of cognition are insufficient to enact the new festival in the soul. We need Mary's female forces of receptivity and compassion, humility and devotion, prayer and intelligence of heart for Sophia to be born in our soul that has become a spiritualized consciousness-soul. Then social community building forces can be active.

On this religious soil we can humanize social life through the Social Impulse of Anthroposophy, and it can receive a new sacramental character as in the old mysteries. We may assume that the future religion will increasingly take place in social life. On November 27, 1916, Rudolf Steiner said that professions become sacramental again when deeds become service, service to the Godhead, when we live in the consciousness that Christ is behind us in everything we do.[86] This can fundamentally alter professional life for a teacher, for example, a curative educator, farmer or physician. It means that Christ forces will work through them and Christ is teaching, healing and working on the earth.

Sacramentalism is Uriel's sphere, and this stream has not yet developed clearly defined professions. It is still in preparation, and their development relates to a growing consciousness of the social impulse. In principle, every profession, every human activity, can acquire priestly, sacramental characteristics. Steiner, for example, held his last course on the cooperation of physicians and ministers, the so-called "pastoral medicine course".[87] Many aspects of pastoral work have already been integrated in social work in the course of the 20th century. In the conversations Steiner had with people, he often acted as a pastoral counselor to them, as the collection of

---

86  Rudolf Steiner: *The Karma of Vocation* (1916), New York 1984 (CW 172).

87  Rudolf Steiner: *Broken Vessels,* Great Barrington 2003 (CW 318).

personal memories published by the German Christian Community priest Wolfgang Gädeke shows.[88]

A lay priesthood that helps others on their paths of development forms in the Uriel stream. It can be biography-work and biographical psychological counseling, accompanying people with developmental problems, partnership counseling, accompaniment of young people who want to discover and develop abilities, support of the process of dying, and being a buddy for AIDS-patients, to name a few. It can also lead to mutual friendship, carrying, supporting and mirroring our paths of development. On the social level professions appear, such as social worker, mediator, consultant for companies and new initiatives. These relatively new professions and non-professional forms of accompaniment and human relationships from the Uriel stream have certain characteristics:

- They are concerned with co-carrying the karma of others without wanting to change them. In the area of the social impulse we ought to take the other person as they are, wrote Dieter Brüll in an essay on Urielites from 1989 in his book *Creating Social Sacraments*.[89]
- We can help make the personal karma of others understandable and visible so that it can be ordered and harmonized. Ahriman makes karma chaotic in our time, but Christ can amplify for the well-being of humanity what we balance karmically.
- Human soul processes can be activated again in the Urielic activity of conversation. Many people are stuck in their development of soul and they do not have access to the spiritual world and spiritual experiences. When openness to the spirit vanishes, a completely new religious-social access to nurturing the life of soul must be found.

---

88  Wolfgang Gädeke: *Viel mehr als nur die Antwort auf meine Frage – Rudolf Steiner als Seelsorger*, Stuttgart 2016.

89  Dieter Brüll: *Creating Social Sacraments*, AWSNA, Wilton 2019.

- We can support the healing of the heart forces that suffered from the intellectualism of modern culture and modern man's egoism. The regeneration of the heart can be achieved by a new social consciousness that helps us to ignite the "inner Sun" of Christ in our heart. Uriel's name can then mean the "Light of Christ" that can shine through us into the social world.
- We can re-create the social processes and forms we live and work in so that a sphere of rights can arise. Social paths of development become visible, and the social impulse can be active wherever people gather.
- There are new forms of conflict resolution in which socially sensitive people play a mediating role. These can be referees, but also people who in a mediation reunite the partners in the conflict and solve the dispute in a sensible way, making arrangements that are right for all persons, such as in a divorce situation.
- The etheric and astral space between people and in groups is repeatedly occupied by the forces of the double. There are people with conversational ability who can cleanse these spaces and heal social relationships.

The heart-path of the social impulse, related to Manichaeism and leading to the ignition of the "inner Sun", is based on practice in everyday life; for it is only here that we can learn to be social. This social path of development represents an immediate path to Christ, a path to the imitation of Christ that begins with the washing of the feet, the service to the other.

The Middle Ages knew a mystical path of initiation, the awakening of the feelings that Christ lived through on His path. This Christian path of feeling that requires seclusion from the world for years is hardly possible any longer, nor can the modern initiation of Anthroposophy bring it back. Today's path is the developmental path of the social impulse. The social world, rather than the hermit's hut, is the place where heart forces are purified in community. This modern path of social life, leading to consciousness of Christ's presence in our heart and the hearts of others, passes through sacrifice and suffering and makes our heart sensitive to how people treat each other. Valentin Tomberg described Steiner's life as a path of suffering along the Stations of the Cross. It is Steiner's path in social life in an uncomprehending environment that ridiculed and attacked his deepest impulses.

Russian culture carries the idea of Christ as human brother whom we meet in a suffering fellow human being. Our path in social life constantly brings us into contact with Christ, but we are barely conscious of it as yet and do not experience it in our heart. What we do to others in our inadequacies, we indeed do to Christ. Therefore, every person making somebody else suffer causes a new path of suffering for Christ. Dieter Brüll perceived a possibility for a new Christian path of feeling when we experience the new Passion of Christ.[90] Medieval mystics awakened feelings of the historical Passion of Christ and could experience initiation through these feelings. Today's social impulse can ignite on suffering with others, and gain strength in experiencing the Passion that humanity causes Christ to suffer in modern times. In the future we will be able to experience the social world as the world of Christ's suffering and this experience will bring us into His sphere. Out of this feeling and suffering with Christ and the consciousness that He suffers with us, new forces to stand in social life in a new way can be born in us as a gift from Christ.

In the Anthroposophical Society in Rotterdam, the Netherlands (winter of 1938/39), Tomberg proposed in a series of lectures on the appearance of Christ in the etheric, that these new forces are

---

90   Ibid.

a reversal of Christ's suffering on the Path of the Cross.[91] They are karmic consequences of His crucifixion that are active from the 20th century on. By having been judged, Christ can awaken conscience in us to become judges over ourselves. His scourging made it possible for Him to give comfort and courage for new deeds. The crowning with thorns is reversed into giving us tasks of love. Bearing the cross now heals our desiccated etheric bodies so that we may develop a rich inner life and gain strength to bear our own cross and to eventually help carry the cross of others. Finally, through the crucifixion, Christ grants us a new etheric clairvoyance so that we know what we do to others, to harmonize karma and to see the karmic consequences of our deeds.

New forces of social life can stream to us through our union with the suffering Christ in our heart. Then we can experience Him as "Lord of Karma" who makes sure that the greatest possible human well-being can be created for the rest of earth development through the way we balance karmic debts, as Rudolf Steiner pointed out on December 2, 1911.[92]

In this chapter we have examined the social aspects of the "knowledge cult" and the social qualities of Uriel that we need for our work in the mystery centers of the social world. Since the end of the 19th century the spiritual world has manifested itself in the social world and in our private world. In order to find our way in the mystery drama of our lives, we need abilities that we can acquire by following an individual path of schooling, as described by Rudolf Steiner. In addition, we need a social path of schooling in order to be able to meet others and thereby also to experience a stronger connection with our higher Self. We then learn to cooperate better with each

---

91  Valentin Tomberg: *The Four Sacrifices of Christ and the Appearance of Christ in the Etheric*, Spring Valley 1983.

92  Rudolf Steiner: *Esoteric Christianity and the Mission of Christian Rosenkreutz* (1911-1912), London 1984 (CW 130).

other, to develop a consciousness of rights and to go with each other on a path of social development that leads to new professions.

In the next chapter we will discuss how we can form communities with this new individual and social consciousness, which arise if we take the Social Impulse of Anthroposophy seriously. Then we can create cultural islands out of spiritual initiatives, where new mysteries can blossom in the conscious contact with the spiritual world and where the intentions which Rudolf Steiner connected with Anthroposophy can be realized.

CHAPTER V

# THE CREATION OF COMMUNITIES

## 1. Community building

In the 20th century it has become more difficult to accomplish cooperation. In associating with groups or initiatives we experience many disappointments through conflicts and disconnection in social life. Communities that have been built on tradition increasingly fall apart as we lean more towards individualism. Old instinctive social forces vanish and egoistic forces appear in their place. The inner and social worlds lose their community building supports.

Communities used to be carried by soul forces that unconsciously united people, but individual consciousness increased since the late Middle Ages, first expressing itself in egoism. The individual now turns to instinctive self-assertion and unsocial drives that lead to a battle for survival, a "war of all against all", if social forces are not consciously developed. Attempts to maintain old and create new communities through manipulating unconscious soul forces are inappropriate for our time and evoke forces that destroy self-consciousness, as did the development of Bolshevism and Fascism in the early 20th century. We must recognize that the ordering of social forces from the sphere of the Father God retreated in the 20th century, and now only community building forces from the sphere of Christ can renew social life.

What communities are we talking about? Everywhere where people connect, community emerges. This can be between two persons, in a family, within a circle of friends, at work with colleagues, in our neighborhood. A company can develop into a community, but communities are also formed in cultural life. If we do this with awareness, they come to life and positive spiritual beings can connect with them.

The Social Impulse of Anthroposophy is the instrument developed by Rudolf Steiner for this purpose. Not all of its elements need to be relevant to the community we want to form. In today's culture of the consciousness soul, the individual develops. In the Slavic culture of the future, the community will be central. This needs to be prepared so that eventually, as the highest form of community, the family of mankind will emerge.

Like all movements that try to unite people in a new conscious way to realize certain goals, and then end up splitting apart, the Anthroposophical movement suffered from splintering as well. It has to develop a new connection with the spiritual world in preparation for the spiritual life of a new cultural epoch. We need new social forms.

Most Anthroposophists know only the path of Anthroposophical community building. It leads to the creation of a cognition community that is not yet a social community. We have already seen that it must be united with the social path of development if communities are to arise where culture is renewed with the help of inspirations from the spiritual world. It is not only concerned with the conscious application of the archetypal phenomenon of communication and certain qualities of soul, social attitudes and virtues, but is part of a very definite Anthroposophical Social Impulse. This impulse embraces the necessary elements to build new communities and helps birth the new mysteries, in which we can consciously communicate with inspiring spiritual beings.

With this all-encompassing social path, revealed step by step by Steiner, we can consciously build communities in today's chaos; they need not be Anthroposophical at all. First, it concerns conditions that are appropriate to the times and can be fulfilled by creating an image of the community we want to build, and by applying the four elements of the Anthroposophical Social Impulse: the two laws, a conscious application of the archetypal phenomenon of social life, and the establishment of threefold social conditions. Secondly, it concerns new inner connections between people that are created by fulfilling these conditions.

We can summarize the meaning of these four elements for community building as follows: The Fundamental Sociological Law and the Fundamental Social Law relate to the spiritual and economic aspects of community building. New communities should serve the free development of individual members. Communities must be set up according to the Fundamental Sociological Law for people to unfold their needs and abilities in a free spiritual life. Through the implementation of the Fundamental Social Law, the separation of labor and income will gradually increase the well-being of the group of cooperating people. Work can become a gift we give with joy to another who needs our services. The community must then provide the possibility of livelihood and grant income to each member. In cooperation we have to speak about money and income openly.

We can still barely apply the archetypal phenomenon of communication with consciousness, but with practice it is a future possibility. It allows us to perceive the other human being in his or her needs and understand what lives in them. Without the concrete practice of our skills of conversation it is impossible to find mutual understanding, to establish relations of rights and duties, and to connect individual impulses. With the archetypal phenomenon of social life, we can awaken "in" each other: for example, we can discover our inner nature because somebody listens with deep interest. Conversation can awaken our higher nature and release social forces and impulses.

Social threefolding can shape our social relationships in community as long as we are not yet inwardly social. This can be achieved by creating a sphere of rights between spiritual and economic aspects of life in which decisions are made together and in equality; where mandates are given and rights and obligations mutually decided. Individuals have the possibility of self-education, of holding what they have agreed to. We are often involuntarily educated when we have too little consciousness in our behavior towards others in social life. Aspects of doubles can lead to conflicts and confrontations with others. Through social threefolding we can lessen the impact of these conflicts and remove them from the inter-human sphere by providing the appropriate social forms and rules that can educate us. Conflicts will not go away but they will be constructive and educational. This is the case when threefolding grows organically out of a consciousness of rights, not when introduced as scheme.

We need a new element to build a community on even deeper spiritual foundations. If Steiner had remained on earth, he could possibly have done this in 1926, seven years after he wrote his book about social threefolding. People associating in community need to order their relationships because we have karmic links with some, and with others we create new connections. Steiner spoke of the need to harmonize karma as a condition of developing the Society of the Christmas Conference. We could say to each other: "Let us try to get along and cooperate, although we are different and may even have been enemies in past lives." The next element of the social impulse would relate to transforming old into new karma and begin the conscious building of a karmic community. When such an ordering of karma happens, the conditions would be fulfilled that Steiner connected with the success of the Christmas Conference in 1923.

On the social path we can create relationships more consciously. We may discover that we belong to certain karmic circles and form new links in freedom. Each meeting can change our destiny, but we are often not awake enough to understand its importance. We sleep through the possibilities of getting to know others and ourselves and miss opportunities of community with people who could be midwives of our higher nature.

We can solve conflicts with certain people and deepen relationships with others when we increase consciousness for what takes place in meetings. Our loving interest for what lives in the soul of others and compassion and attention for how they face their destiny is the prerequisite. Images of others and of their karmic circumstances can arise when we open up to them; we can be inwardly touched and spiritually activated. Human community grows out of what we co-create. Past karma can gradually turn fruitful. Negative forces are transformed, positive forces come to us from others and new karma is created.

To experience the process of community building concretely and consciously and strengthen human relationships in existing communities, it helps to give special meetings and gatherings a festive, cultic character. This was and is the custom in Eastern Europe when a guest (perceived as sent by God) joined a meal, for example. Rituals can help to bring new consciousness to the importance of meetings. In every human being we can meet Christ, the Lord of Karma, who multiplies the effect of deeds in service to others. As a new element of the Anthroposophical Social Impulse, this could raise forming karmic communities to consciousness. The community would then develop its own etheric organism, protect its members and relate to the spiritual world as center for the new mysteries.

The weekly Bible evening, created by Karl König in Camphill communities, can be understood from this perspective. The heart of each community member can open to the presence of Christ in these evenings. This social form allows us to increasingly experience karmic community in which people carry each other's inadequacies and karma. We enter the sphere of the Greater Guardian. Hans Muller-Wiedemann describes in his biography of Karl König the Bible evening. He quotes:

> Every Saturday evening each house community gathers–where and what their work may be–to prepare for Sunday. Members gather around a table, have a simple meal, speak about events of the past week and then turn to the Gospel that will be read on Sunday. Everyone is expected to prepare for the Bible evening in the course of the week and invited to relate to the friends the experiences of reading and thinking about the Gospel.[93]

When karma is harmonized to an appropriate level in community, it creates an atmosphere in which Christ can be experienced. This happens in a "social etheric" temple. The Anthroposophical movement could have achieved this, again seven years later, in 1933 when, according to Steiner, Christ would reappear in the etheric sphere of the earth. Even though the Anthroposophical movement

---
93  Hans Müller-Wiedemann: *Karl König*, Camp Hill Books 1996.

in general cannot create these conditions, groups can sometimes for a short moment experience the healing and comforting presence of Christ and receive inspirations through other spiritual beings.

The Anthroposophical Social Impulse thus leads to special karmic communities in which people take others into their being and draw their strength from each other, where spiritual beings can descend and act through individuals. This is a Manichean social form of Christian life where new social forces can be active between people. It is an image of a future life. We cannot yet consciously unite in this form because of the lack of heart forces which still need to be developed. In the Slavic culture of the future these conditions might be fulfilled.

Through education and practice we can build communities on the Manichean path of the social impulse to create foundations for a new spiritual culture that is prepared in the new mysteries. Manichaeism's role in developing a new culture is almost completely overlooked in the Anthroposophical movement, and this has led to neglect and misunderstanding of the social impulse. Nevertheless, Manichean impulses are indispensable for creating a new spiritual life.

Mani was executed in 276 AD in the Iranian city of Gondishapur. His stream was little known in history. The Bogumils from the Balkan, the Patarenes of Italy, the Cathars and Waldensians from the south of France and the Templars belong to it. It had branches in the Dutch Brethren of Common Life, the movement of Beguines of Rhineland and the Bohemian-Moravian brothers and sisters of the Czech countries. They combined spiritual life with a life devoted to care for others. We can also find Manichaean in the building lodges of Medieval cathedrals.

On November 11, 1911, Rudolf Steiner described the connecting link between all these groups as the cultivation of the outer form of life, the attempt to develop forms of community that can receive a future Christian life.[94] Among them we find communities where an original, apostolic Christianity developed. These were concerned with hallowing and healing social life that took place in small congregations. Each member, as lay priest, could develop a pure attitude towards others and the spiritual world. In a broad sense, Manichaeans work to redeem evil through gentleness, and help people on their paths of development and in their needs.

The Manichean stream builds "social etheric" temples as cultivator of the outer form of life. The Aristotelians and the Platonists still have to learn this. In this sense the Anthroposophical Social Impulse can be understood as a new impulse to build a "social etheric" temple in the inter-human etheric sphere. Each of its elements displays Manichean motifs. We can develop new social forms with the Fundamental Sociological Law to help individuals on their way. The Fundamental Social Law can lead to social forms where work becomes a gift to others. The archetypal phenomenon of communication can teach us to take the other into our consciousness and bring his or her spirit to awakening. It can be mutual, or more one-sided in a therapeutic process. With social threefolding we create the social form in which people can relinquish their claims to power and create conditions of rights based on an acceptance of the peculiarity and dignity of the other. This can lead to the building of a karmic community where people unite karmically in freedom and take each other into their hearts to build a social temple out of heart forces.

These karmic links arise in spirit-awakening conversations as they took place with Rudolf Steiner and Ita Wegman, and can also take place in a community. These connections arise in phases. They protect the participants and invite spiritual beings to descend and unite. We are in need of modern Manicheans who develop new forms

---

94   Rudolf Steiner: *The Temple Legend* (1904-1914), London 1985 (CW 93).

of social work and social healing to bring karma to consciousness and harmonize it in new communities.

On September 11, 1910, Steiner pointed out that the karma of the individual must connect itself with the karma of groups. A community can help carry the karma of an individual, which means that others or a whole community can help carry the consequences of the negative actions of an individual.[95] In early Christian communities people could confess their sins in public and ask the community to help them carry the consequences. Carrying karma together is a Manichean principle.

Liturgy creates a community where the cultic form allows spiritual beings to descend into the social space. This community is like a gift from above. In contrast, the path of community building through the Social Impulse of Anthroposophy asks us to consciously build a "social etheric" temple in the community for spiritual beings to enter and meet and inspire people. Such temples of the new mysteries in a karmic community built after the Manichean model provide the possibility for a new culture to arise as the fruit of these meetings. In their friendship Rudolf Steiner and Ita Wegman built a "social etheric" temple in which they could do their spiritual research.

"Social etheric" temples are the mystery centers where the School for Spiritual Science that Rudolf Steiner wanted to create can work in everyday life. The School, founded at the Christmas Conference of 1923, was to be realized in karmic communities. As mystery school, it was also given from above. To create the appropriate conditions for its future functioning, we need social temples in which the fount of Anthroposophy can flow from below upwards in our spiritual work. Culture islands can then arise that renew culture and build a bridge to the future.

We can summarize this process of community building by presenting the development of its different aspects as a learning process

---

95  Rudolf Steiner: *The Gospel of Matthew* (1910), London 1965 (CW 123).

of seven steps that do not necessarily have a fixed order. We can imagine this process by taking the example of the community in the family. The steps in its development seem easy, but in practice they are difficult. We are allowed to make mistakes, we are not yet perfect. With our good intentions it should be possible to solve conflicts and by doing this purify the "social etheric" space, and to gradually transform the problematic aspects of our double. The stages of this small learning process may give us inspiration for the creation of larger communities. According to the social impulse of Anthroposophy these steps are as follows:

1. Community building starts with creating an image of the new community. In 1891, Rudolf Steiner found this image in the *Fairytale of the Green Snake and the Beautiful Lily* by Goethe. A snake lives in an underground temple and sacrifices herself to create a bridge between two worlds, and as a result a temple arises out of the earth.
2. A community can become a community for development. It should serve the development of individuals that constitute the community, as Steiner formulated in 1898 in the Fundamental Sociological Law. In such a community people can support each other in their development.
3. A community can become a work community, where the well-being of the whole depends on the degree of separation of labor and income, as Steiner stated in 1905 in the Fundamental Social Law. All practical affairs of the community, including questions of money, should be taken into careful consideration.
4. A community can become a place of meeting where people try to consciously apply the archetypal phenomenon of communication. In real communication people can awaken each other and discover the meaning of love for a new social life as Steiner described in 1912.

5. A community can become a community of rights. It needs the principle of social threefolding for a healthy structure, as Steiner presented in his book of 1919.
6. A community can become a karmic community in which people learn to live with each other's imperfections and cooperate fruitfully. Such a community arises when people commit themselves to work on certain tasks together.
7. A community can become a "social etheric" temple, a mystery center where communication with the spiritual world is possible. In this community people can create a new culture of love and brotherhood.

Each of these steps requires a sacrifice that overcomes a part of our egoism. These sacrifices transform our doubles and connect our higher beings with each other. In every community that follows this path, there are seven tasks that can be performed by different people:

1. Creating a common vision and formulation of tasks
2. Ensuring the development of all the members
3. Perceiving the needs of the members
4. Deepening the ability to communicate
5. Preventing the exercise of uncontrolled power
6. Solving conflicts and ordering karma
7. Guarding and cultivating the "social etheric" space

## 2. Culture Islands

When Steiner held the agricultural course in Koberwitz (now Poland) on Whitsun 1924, he spoke about Germany's future during a dinner conversation and said:

The chimneys [of industry] will topple and Germany will sink to an agricultural state ... It will be a matter of creating islands of monastic seclusion in the countryside where German cultural and spiritual life can still be cultivated ... Foreign countries will send their sons and daughters to be educated there.[96]

This would require the creation of centers of spiritual life where Anthroposophy can live and flourish. After the Second World War, the American Morgenthau Plan of August 1944, in fact, envisioned a future scenario of German economy in a structure of agriculture and small businesses. It was abandoned, and from 1947 on German economy was rebuilt to curb Russian expansion.

As a result, a technocratic society arose, subordinating spiritual life to economy instead of an agricultural society with spiritual oases. European Anthroposophical institutions are endangered by this increasing technocratic regulation of society. Until recently Anthroposophists were happy when their institution was accepted by the state. Today we know that recognition is usually linked to consequences that place it under technocratic control and place it in danger of losing its Anthroposophical identity.

In modern society freedom of spiritual life vanishes and the path to the spirit becomes increasingly difficult for individuals. In the European Union, digital education will be obligatory in all schools, ministries of education determine what children need to learn, and the production and sale of Anthroposophical and homeopathic remedies are becoming increasingly difficult because their effects cannot be proven in terms of materialistic science. Children's vaccinations are becoming mandatory in more and more countries and in connection with the Corona epidemic Bill Gates and others are already talking about worldwide mandatory vaccinations against all diseases. This could then be registered with a subcutaneous chip.

---
96   Adalbert von Keyserlingk (ed.): *The Birth of a New Agriculture - Koberwitz 1924*, London 2009.

In our materialistic society spiritual life has to find a new orientation in a declining culture. If the Anthroposophical movement wants to survive it has to concentrate in centers where a conscious connection with the spiritual world can be developed in the new mysteries. For these centers I use the image of "culture islands". The impulse to build therapeutic centers as culture islands in every city where people can be healed in an all-encompassing way, lived strongly in Ita Wegman. We can also think of schools, farms, and other kinds of spiritual centers. A home community or a family can also be an island of culture from where spiritual inspirations and impulses radiate out into the surrounding areas.

Such islands of a new spiritual culture can arise out of a process of community building based on the Anthroposophical Social Impulse. This process not only includes people who are directly involved, but also the larger community they want to serve, such as clients of therapeutic centers, parents of children, consumers, and other interested persons. This larger community that is open to spiritual impulses does not have to be Anthroposophical.

Many Anthroposophical institutions are not communities in the sense of this social impulse and are only to a certain extent islands of culture. They have the usual hierarchical structure and are tied to state funds and state control. Their Anthroposophical identity is often not deeply rooted, because, for example, many employees in Waldorf schools or in institutions of curative pedagogy have no deep connection with Anthroposophy. Anthroposophy has become a method. If they can restructure and deepen their Anthroposophical identity, if the links between people carrying the institutions can be further developed into conscious connections of karma, then islands of culture can arise where people can work together with spiritual beings and deceased ones. For this they have to learn how to perform the "knowledge cult" in the group conversation and to discover the practice of the new mysteries in the "social etheric" temples.

The paths to cultural islands are hardly researched in the Anthroposophical movement. Much is still unclear and unfinished. The social impulse of Anthroposophy was not understood as a path of community building, and social threefolding was not recognized as a means to break structures of power. The threefold structure of the Society that should have been created after the Christmas Conference of 1923 was not realized. The School for Spiritual Science remained incomplete and could not develop into the esoteric center of the new mysteries. Mutual paths of research remain largely unknown, and many Anthroposophists do not have a concrete image of the new mysteries inaugurated at the Christmas Conference.

Even though the new mystery sciences could not develop properly, many people already have certain experiences in the sphere of the new mysteries. These are not only Anthroposophists, for they do not have a monopoly on them. All of humanity can experience a new relationship with the spiritual world in new mysteries, and it should be practiced in the Anthroposophical movement. We must maintain consciousness when we enter the spiritual world and then the group can form the organs with which to perceive it. Individual initiation and spiritual research will not vanish, but group work will in future be an important new path to the realm of the spirit. We must carry consciousness into the world of night through individual exercises, but it will be important to broaden consciousness for the inter-human world as well.

The spiritual world begins to speak when we build proper forms in social life, where we ask questions of each other in karmic communities and allow spiritual experiences in conversation. Of course, we must be awake enough to understand and hold them. It requires a consciousness soul where male and female qualities are integrated and balanced. Each should sacrifice their authority and offer their abilities to others in service. Thus Steiner became Wegman's helper in founding the new medicine. The more highly developed person becomes the servant of the lesser developed.

Insights, not due to individual effort but suddenly falling from the spiritual world, can happen during conversation in a group that tries to solve problems or develop new ideas. It can be a group of teachers discussing a child, physicians and therapists consulting about a patient, a project group investigating a problem, but also parents speaking about problems of raising children. The participants combine their perceptions, each gains perspectives from the others, we think the thoughts of others and suddenly someone may say what summarizes the picture and offers a solution. Maybe the helpful thoughts come from somebody of whom we would not expect this at all. On these paths of research and by asking questions we can experience the new mysteries on a small scale when individuals can speak certain intuitions, and the whole group forms in the mirror of each soul. We can speak of healing social relationships when the strength of the individual soul also lives in the community. These two perspectives form the motto of social ethics that Rudolf Steiner gave to Edith Maryon in 1920.

People who work together in this healing way can concentrate on certain tasks in karmic communities. They can be schools, therapeutic centers, scientific institutes, educational centers or communities of people living together. A culture island can arise when we try to bring something of importance to develop in the world. Two people can already form a culture island and cooperate to solve certain problems by cultivating the connection to the spiritual world. Any group can build a culture island with Anthroposophists and non-Anthroposophists working together. It is decisive that the members of the group are willing to develop together. Increasingly, these culture islands will be of help to people who seek support in the present chaos and need of soul, who want to find new paths of development. Culture islands are lighthouses for those in search of new spirituality in a declining culture, but also for the spiritual world that seeks communities through which it can act.

The Anthroposophical movement can fulfill its task as movement of cultural renewal if it continues to found culture islands in all areas. It can only do so with people who have inwardly developed Anthroposophy to the degree that they can work practically with it; people who have gone the path from the old to the new mysteries. It is here that we come to know Anthroposophy in three aspects: namely, the Father, Son and Holy Spirit.

Anthroposophy appears as teachings and as a world view in the Father aspect; as Christian Theosophy and as a summary of the old mysteries of wisdom acquired under the guidance of a spiritual father. The principles of hierarchy and authority reign and must be transformed. If we fail to do so we find fundamentalism, dogmatism, centralism, sectarianism and a group spirit. Anthroposophy then hardens into a subculture, allowing certain attitudes, habits, traditions and behaviors from the 1920s to continue. They represent the caricatures of Anthroposophy that live in the outside world.

The aspect of the Son is connected to freedom. Here Anthroposophy is the "consciousness of true humanity". I like to call it the consciousness of the renewing, healing activity of Christ in the soul of man (in the inter-human sphere and nature as well). Christ's activity leads to the soul's transformation with a new center in the heart for the being Anthropo-Sophia to live in. Anthroposophy, as developed by Rudolf Steiner, offers much help: the six exercises for the heart chakra, the evening exercise of the retrogressive overview of the day, the path of *The Philosophy of Freedom* and a new approach to artistic and religious experiences.

On this path of transforming the soul we can experience the Spirit aspect of Anthroposophy. When we communicate and cooperate in a spirit of love, Anthroposophy appears as spiritual science, a path of cognition that leads to spiritual knowledge on new paths of common research. The Holy Spirit is active between people from the inside out. Then we are in the sphere of the new mysteries, where Anthroposophy is a living experience of the spiritual world we share and practice with others in karmic communities. Theosophical esotericism becomes living spirituality that is activated when we bring Christ's healing forces in us to consciousness in social life and in nature: in pedagogy, therapy, social work, agriculture, medicine or the manufacturing of remedies. Someone inspired in practical work by Anthroposophy in this sense is an Anthroposophist. Now we can understand a remark Steiner made in 1922 to young people: "Esotericism is action," he said, "action out of concrete impulses from the spiritual world."

The path from old to new mysteries does not only lead to individual transformational processes. The institutional frame of the old mysteries was fundamentally transformed in the new mysteries as well. The Society founded in 1923 was meant as the entrance court to real spiritual activity. We should very simply (without references) become members to get to know Anthroposophy. We should nurture the life of soul so that each could transform and develop a new consciousness, new social forces and impulses. We should unite with others and develop these forces in concrete areas with groups or initiatives.

Through membership in the School for Spiritual Science we can take part in spiritual research and carry responsibility for Anthroposophical work in the world. Sections for different areas of work were created, and Steiner intended to lead them via section leaders. At the time of his death the social section was still missing. The Anthroposophical Social Impulse as basis for any community building in institutions should be the focus of its research. It could realize the spiritual impulses of the other sections in Anthroposophical social forms.

The School, as Steiner conceptualized it, would appear as a spiritual center of a modern order, the Order of Michael, with departments in sections. Each section was to have its esoteric path of training, and possibly an esoteric cult as well. We have the image of a future order where each culture island is a transformed monastery with a lay priesthood serving humanity in freedom. Steiner spoke of a new priesthood in contrast to the ecclesiastic cult priesthood. A new mystery culture appears that is cultivated by groups that build "social etheric" temples in Manichean forms of community, not in outer temples. Now the spiritual world does not act out of secluded mysteries anymore but unites with karmic communities all over the world.

What Steiner brought to earth in the archetypal image of a threefold society whose creation was initiated during the Christmas Conference of 1923 soon became a spiritual wreck. This image has to become reality again out of his original intentions.

## 3. The Social Intentions of Rudolf Steiner

This book is written in memory of the Society of the Christmas Conference of 1923, whose members were made members of the administrative Society in 1925. This putting out of action of the spiritual Society resulted in the disappearance of the sphere in which the life of the soul could be consciously cultivated. Since then, the seeds of a new culture, planted by Steiner, have not been able to grow for a long time. And for the member groups it became difficult to transform old forces of soul.

Steiner's social intentions were not clear to the participants of the Christmas Conference of 1923, and we cannot hold it against them. A mystery drama filled with disastrous conflicts followed, during the course of which the Society collapsed in 1935. Since the middle of the 1950s, and again in the 1980s, in a rhythm of 33 years since 1923, Anthroposophists have sought a path from old to new mysteries. Thus, in 1960, the excluded British and Dutch Anthroposophical Societies united again with the Dornach Society. In the 21st century we can perceive a new impulse that wants to lead the Anthroposophical movement to the new mysteries again.

This new impulse includes attempts to develop new social structures in Anthroposophical institutions and initiatives so that they can continue as culture islands and prepare a new spiritual culture in a technocratic society. The structural principles of cooperation in spiritual groups that Steiner wanted to realize in the Society of the Christmas Conference are clarified again. They are appropriate to self-consciousness as it should be developed in the age of Michael. This Society represented the archetypal image of a free and future cooperation of people. Battles of power, authoritarian and hierarchical structures that still exist in every spiritual circle and community must be overcome. Steiner's social vision is of great importance to any group that wants to renew spiritual, political and economic life.

Over the years groups in the Anthroposophical movement have discovered qualities of the new mysteries and new insights have been born. Many assumed that this depended on social processes in these groups or possibilities to awaken "on" each other and to be awakened by others in encounters. Some people know that a new spiritual life can only take place in new social forms. Others discovered that new social forces must be born within ourselves before we can associate in the sense of the new mysteries. What Rudolf Steiner developed in the Society from outside, from the spiritual world, can now be conquered again in freedom and from within by the inner activity of the members of the Anthroposophical movement.

The burning of the first Goetheanum, Steiner's early death, a missing successor for the School and dismantling the Society that was founded in 1923 are clear indications that everything from the outside and above had to fall away, to be born again from the inside and from below. We can spiritually and socially rebuild the Goetheanum in our practical work. Steiner disappeared as outer authority, but he remained spiritually accessible to people who want to unite with the spiritual world out of their own strength. The spiritual Society of 1923 can arise again between people who want to take the path to the new mysteries. The School for Spiritual Science can be rebuilt again from below by people's cooperation so that the spirit is activated between them. Social threefolding has to be won from below in the same sense, out of the experiences and catastrophes of modern social life. The Representative of Man, Steiner's Christ statue, was to be visible to all in the first Goetheanum. It was consequently hidden in a secondary room of the second Goetheanum before it was made visible again.

When Rudolf Steiner became president of the Anthroposophical Society at the Christmas Conference, the Society and its daughter movements that developed since the end of the First World War, were able to unite. The Society was to carry the whole Anthroposophical movement, the Michael movement, as it exists in the spiritual world. It united in Steiner's personality and was to gradually merge in practice with the threefold structure of the new Society. On January 13, 1924, Steiner wrote in the Newsletter of the Society:

"The statutes of the Christmas Conference [are] the basic lines of action for the realization of the Anthroposophical Society as the form that the heavenly Anthroposophical movement, i.e. the new Christianity, needs for its care on earth."

The daughter movements, as they live in areas of practice, represents the Society's will pole oriented to current issues. The School is the thinking pole where spiritual research should take place and solutions to current issues can be worked out. The member groups form the heart where the whole of what lives in the practical work can flow together, where, through nurturing the life of soul the social and spiritual forces for the new mysteries can be created.

## 4. The Rebirth of Anthroposophy

After 1968 (which is 2 x 33 years after 1902, when Steiner became active in the Theosophical Society) a wave of Michaelic impulses went across the world. This led to the rise of human rights movements , the Peace movements, the Green movements. This brought new life into the Anthroposophical work as well. Waldorf schools were founded in many countries, Anthroposophical medicine flourished and the number of bio-dynamical farms continued to grow. Other kinds of Anthroposophical work developed or were initiated. This led, 21 years later, from the end of the 1980s (2 x 33 years after the conference of Christmas 1923) until the end of the 20th century to a certain culmination of Anthroposophy worldwide. The American Anthroposophist Stephen E. Usher mentioned the year 2002.[97] Since the end of the 20th century the membership of the General Anthroposophical Society is declining.

At the end of the 20th century Anthroposophy did not become the cultural factor Rudolf Steiner had envisioned it to be, but we can say that Anthroposophical initiatives worldwide are doing wonderful things in modern culture, and reach millions of people. In the summer of 1924 Steiner spoke about the cooperation of Platonists from the School of Chartres, and Aristotelians at the turn of the millennium. He indicated its dependency on the continued impulse of the

---

97  Stephen E. Usher, "Remarks on the Culmination at the End of the 20th Century", in: *Jupiter*, Vol. 6/2, December 2011.

Christmas Conference and "whether the Anthroposophical Society knows how to cultivate Anthroposophy in an appropriately devoted way," as he said on July 18, 1924.[98] This common Platonic-Aristotelian work should lead to a certain culmination of Anthroposophy, but this collaboration did not take place in the sense anticipated by Steiner. It may come later. Spiritual development has taken a completely different direction after 1933.

In his opening lecture at the Michael Conference in 2000, Manfred Schmidt-Brabant, then chairman of the General Anthroposophical Society, asked some unexpected questions:

"Isn't there something upon Anthroposophy, after all, like an occult prison? Let us look at its effectiveness to the outside world. Despite all the institutions, endless work in lectures and courses, we get stuck as if in a ghetto. We do not get out, to the extent that, according to its significance, Anthroposophy should have become effective in the world long ago. And isn't there also this occult imprisonment within? ... Is it not as if the walls are erected between people? One looks at so many inquiring, industrious, fruitful, intelligent people ... and it is not possible that they join together to form working communities."[99]

These were important questions. Anthroposophy is not really coming into the world and Anthroposophists have problems working together. These phenomena are well known. The Michaelic impulses seem to be paralyzed and the social forces are too weak to come to a proper cooperation.

Every spiritual impulse needs a renewal after three times 33 years to be able to incarnate more deeply into culture. Anthroposophy wants to be reborn as a spiritual impulse after a century (maybe

---

98  Rudolf Steiner: *Karmic Relationships,* Vol. 6 (1924), London 1975 (CW 240).

99  Manfred Schmidt-Brabant, "Der Kampf um den ethischen Individualismus", in: *Was in der Anthroposophischen Gesellschaft vorgeht,* Nachrichten für deren Mitglieder, Nr. 39, 23.9.2001.

even under a new name). This implies that all the impulses that developed between 1902 and 1925 will go through a process of renewal. A century after the beginning of Rudolf Steiner's work in the Theosophical Society (1902) a new Anthroposophy wants to be born. She will no longer appear on earth in the garment of theosophical terminology and administered in a hierarchic structure, but as a new spiritual consciousness born directly out of the questions of the time. Steiner indicated that the great Platonists and Aristotelians would be responsible together for the spiritualization of intelligence that is needed in our times. As a platform for this, Steiner had founded the Anthroposophical Society.

At the end of the 20th century, the question of the relationship between the spiritual Society of the Christmas Conference of 1923-24 (the Anthroposophical Society) and the administrative Society (the General Anthroposophical Society) reappeared. In 2000 an official constitution commission of ten people was set up at the General Assembly in Dornach in order to clarify this issue once and for all. After consulting the lawyers Andreas Furrer and Jürgen Erdmenger, the conclusion was reached in 2001 that these were two different societies, which had not merged in 1925. The committee agreed to propose to re-establish the Anthroposophical Society in cooperation with the members. However, this proposal was set aside in 2002 by the board members of the General Anthroposophical Society Paul Mackay and Bodo von Plato, who were also members of the committee, and other functionaries. They came up with their own proposal.

At a conference in Christmas 2002 these functionaries proposed to reanimate the society that had been founded at the Christmas Conference of 1923 (and had already withdrawn into the etheric world in 1925) in the completely outdated form of a centralized society. This proposal was accepted by most of the present members, but after an appeal to the Swiss court this had to be reversed. With this fateful event a century (1902-2002) came to an end, in which the

General Anthroposophical Society in its traditional form has become superfluous for many Anthroposophists. It must reformulate its task.

In 2002 precisely the opposite would have been necessary to take care of Anthroposophy and bring people together. Anthroposophy is a matter of individuals who work out of a spiritual connection with the being Anthropo-Sophia and and take initiatives with each other on that basis. The General Anthroposophical Society only has a right to exist if it supports these initiatives.

New impulses are necessary so that the 100th anniversary of the Christmas Conference of 1923 can be celebrated. On the way to this celebration, in 2019, a rehabilitation of the board members Elisabeth Vreede and Ita Wegman, who had been expelled from the Society in 1935, took place. But deeper social and institutional transformations (more consciousness of rights, a culture of encounter, collegial boards, democratization, decentralization of the Society and the School for Spiritual Science) are necessary so that the seeds sown by Steiner a century ago can properly germinate and flourish after 2023.

In 1992, in his spiritual testament *Battle for the Soul*, the Dutch Anthroposophist Bernard Lievegoed envisioned the end of the 20th century.[100] The anthroposophical impulse is much larger than the Anthroposophical Society and all over the world we find people who develop spiritual science, he said. The new Anthroposophical impulse could issue from a very different angle than Anthroposophists might expect.

New impulses live at the periphery of the Anthroposophical movement. We can find them among young people with artistic and social ideals. These tend to be Platonic souls who find little understanding in an intellectual Aristotelian Anthroposophy. So-called Platonists could also be among them; many have a distinct social-Manichean impulse. They search for openness in conversations and meetings

---

[100] Bernard Lievegoed: *Battle for the Soul*, Stroud 1996.

in their initiatives and groups, and look for answers to questions of life. They seek their own inner Anthroposophy.

There is much more social and spiritual awareness in the world than a century ago. Young people are much more open to spirituality and more sensitive to the suffering of others and of the world. They have grown up in a world of technology that entices them to immerse themselves in a virtual (sub-natural) world of games and social media communication and therefore they lose touch with the human world. Or in a world of synthetic drugs that change their consciousness and give them the false impression of a spiritual journey. In both worlds of this mind jail almost every human being spends some time before they can liberate themselves from it. Among young people it is in most cases a temporary phase from which they can emerge as adults.

Reading a book or watching a movie can set young people on a spiritual journey that changes their lives. *The Lord of the Rings*, the films of Andrei Tarkovski, the *Harry Potter* movies, *The Matrix* trilogy, the books of Paulo Coelho and so many others can convince us that there is a spiritual world, with good and evil spirits, that there is a choice between them which evokes our moral consciousness and our conscience. A wave of awakening among young people spreads over the Internet because of the climate crisis, which makes them understand, at first with their emotions but later also with their minds, that they must save their future.

Thus the spiritual world and the spiritual leaders of humanity, among them Rudolf Steiner, have many opportunities to awaken people and inspire them to act in harmony with the impulses of the Time Spirit Michael. Anthroposophy can be reborn in such ways. This will be related to contemporary issues that are important to young people, such as the meaning of life, working on the human double, dealing with technology, overcoming addictions, mental health issues, paths of schooling, meditation, global challenges, connecting with other people in the formation of our destiny, and community building. The new impulses should now come from younger people.

In the course of the 20th century the social world has increasingly become a mystery center where evil forces are penetrating our consciousness and good forces can be invited to appear. We have to build communities to work with the good forces. The Archangel Michael expects us to be armed for an inner battle against the forces destroying our soul and to found a new spiritual culture in culture islands. These are comprehensive tasks and take decades. We are only at the beginning and do not yet have the social and spiritual forces at our disposal that need to be developed in the next centuries. Modesty and understanding of our own as well as others' inadequacies are necessary. It is still rather difficult, but will become easier for future generations if we try and associate in soul and spirit.

According to an unknown source, Rudolf Steiner said that five to six million individualities were gathered in the cosmic cult that the Archangel Michael led in the spiritual world in the decades around 1800. They look for circles in which a Michaelic spirituality is living. We need not convert them, but find the way to unite them to their deepest impulses in a language they understand. Anthroposophy's old baggage has to go so that it can be recognized and awaken people who want to unite spiritually in the near future. They want to experience a new festival of Whitsun that leads to a conscious relation to Christ's reappearance in the etheric and to a breakthrough to a new spiritual era. All of humanity should take part in this spiritual awakening. It means that the Anthroposophical movement has to seek links to other movements with a Michaelic consciousness. It could show developmental paths appropriate to the times and available to humanity for a new connection to the living Christ and the renewal of culture.

## 5. The Anthroposophical Society

It is a challenge for the General Anthroposophical Society to create the conditions for a new Anthroposophical impulse and the rebirth of the Anthroposophical movement after one century. The question of what can be done here is alive in all national Societies. Anthroposophy has in many ways become a method successfully applied in schools, health care, agriculture and many other areas, but it is only to a limited extent a path of spiritual research. The external successes were accompanied by a loss of spiritual depth.

We find in many countries a growing number of people with an interest in Waldorf education, in Anthroposophical medicine and biodynamic products, but they have no interest in Anthroposophy. This includes many teachers of Waldorf schools, staff of Anthroposophical institutions and students in Anthroposophical studies. However, all these people -- and there are hundreds of thousands of them in the world -- have spiritual questions that could be addressed in new forms of Anthroposophical work.

There are many reasons for the slow growth of the Society after 1925. They have to be taken into consideration when we want to prepare the Society for a new Anthroposophical impulse. Most of these reasons were already part of the difficult birth process of the Society of 1923; others are connected with the culture in which we live at present:

- The failure to order karma. The success of the Christmas Conference and the new Society depended on the ordering of karma among the members. Because this did not take place in 1924, the Conference was a failure, according to Rudolf Steiner himself. There was not enough social consciousness in the Society to solve the conflicts. Powerful group doubles poisoned the "social etheric" space of the Society.

- The early death of Rudolf Steiner. Steiner's illness had different causes. The spiritual world called him back in 1925. Anthroposophy and the School for Spiritual Science remained unfinished.
- A weakness in Michaelic thinking. Steiner mentioned this in relation to the work for social threefolding. This seemed to be a more general weakness in the Society, together with a lack of people with Michaelic courage.
- The rising of the Beast from the abyss. In 1933 humanity would have to face the apocalyptic Beast from the abyss. Nazism was one of its faces. The board of the Society was divided since the death of Steiner and fell apart in 1935. The Society was not ready for the Second Coming of Christ. Only few people recognized the dangers.
- Spiritual pretensions. After Steiner's death the Society lost its connection with the Michael movement. Still, the board of the Society behaved as if they stood in a kind of apostolic succession to him. Anthroposophists may have presented themselves to others as people with higher knowledge, as spiritual elitists.
- The elimination of the female element. Groups have been reading lecture cycles not really appropriate for the soul work that should take place there. This could create an intellectual atmosphere in which the male element dominated. Steiner complained to Polzer-Hoditz about the elimination of the female element from the Society.
- Dogmatism. The texts of Steiner became authoritative. He gave his lectures, however, only for the people who were present. In the beginning he did not want them to be stenographed. When they were published they were heavily edited, so that we do not know what he actually said. For this reason it does not make sense to say: "Dr. Steiner said …"

- The connection with the outside world. In certain respects the Society lost the connection with the modern world. This evil world had to be separated from the Anthroposophical world.
- The decline of German culture. Nazism corrupted the use of German language and made it difficult for Germans to connect with their earlier culture. German ceased to be a language of culture and Anthroposophy suffers from that as well.
- The materialism of daily life. Materialism used to be a way of thinking. In the 20th century it has become a way of life. Everything spiritual is suspect, not only in the eyes of the scientists but also of many others. They do not accept things they cannot see. Also, the Christian religious point of view has largely disappeared from the modern world view.
- Technology. The spiritual needs of modern people are perverted by technology. The need to develop imaginations has been replaced by ready-made virtual images on a screen. With new media our minds are imprisoned by companies who earn their money by captivating our attention. This is a consciousness jail. Technology displaces and replaces spirituality.
- The burdens of modern life. People of working age have less time and energy to attend lectures and seminars, and to read books that are not that easy.

Looking at this list we can understand these reasons very well. It was difficult to transform the old theosophical ways and the intellectual approach of the young scientists. Rudolf Steiner would work in a different way with us now. How the Anthroposophical Society would have to change were he to connect with it again?

The threefold social structure of the Anthroposophical Society, which Steiner designed, was not realized. The centralized social structure that existed at his death was not viable. Marie Steiner and

Albert Steffen understood this immediately after Rudolf Steiner's death. The General Anthroposophical Society should have limited itself to administrative tasks and supporting the initiatives of individuals in their local groups. Instead, it took over the tasks of the spiritual Society and the School, without its board being spiritually competent. Until the 1990s, the board considered itself to be an esoteric board. It still controls the work with the class lessons, although the class texts have been accessible to everyone since 1992. In many countries groups of Anthroposophists are already working independently with these texts in a fruitful way, as a collection of reports from 2019 shows.[101] The School for Spiritual Science can also organize its tasks independently. In this way, the General Anthroposophical Society can limit itself to its essential task.

In my view, such a decentralized structure is the right one for the future, with member groups and initiative groups being inspired by the etheric Anthroposophical Society of 1923, with an autonomous School for Spiritual Science and a General Anthroposophical Society creating the right conditions for the initiatives and connecting them.

We can imagine such a threefold Anthroposophical Society Rudolf Steiner could work with. A Society in which the initiatives of the members are in the centre. A Society that discovers the Social Impulse of Anthroposophy and creates social foundations for its spiritual work. It will then consciously build social communities in which the spirit can live. We can imagine a Society that develops the ideas of Anthroposophy further, in connection with modern spiritual insights. We can imagine a Society in which a consciousness for the activity of group doubles has become normal, a Society of people with Michaelic thoughts and courage, a Society without spiritual pretensions, that is not dogmatic, where the male and the female elements are in balance, a Society that does not offer an intellectual Anthroposophy, but a living, creative, moral, warm, spiritual way of

---

101  Elisabeth Wutte and Günter Röschert (ed.), *Perspektiven freier Hochschularbeit*, Steinbergkirche 2019.

talking about and living with Anthroposophy, a Society that has its place in the world and is respected by the general public. A Society that creates a new spiritual culture that transforms modern materialistic culture and awakens the appropriate moral consciousness for the use of technology. We can also imagine a Society with activities in which people can experience a real regeneration from a busy life.

In many Anthroposophical communities we can see all these aspects, but they have not become general yet. We need a new generation of spiritually inspired pioneers who create a Society with the right conditions for a new Anthroposophy. A Society that leaves the failures and group doubles of the first century of Anthroposophy behind.

It's good to see what the Society of the Christmas Conference should be. In the first article of the statutes of 1923 we read that it is "an association of people whose will it is to nurture the life of the soul, both in the individual and in human society, on the basis of a true knowledge of the spiritual world." The members should consciously place the Foundation Stone of this new Society in their hearts so that they would find within themselves the power to connect "in harmonious cooperation" the work in the world with the deepest spirituality. On this Foundation Stone they could build a spirit temple.

How can a contemporary care of the soul life in man and the world be organized on the basis of a true knowledge of the spiritual world? What can Anthroposophy mean for the modern world? Four levels can be distinguished here:

1. The dissemination of a new art of living. A century ago it was easier to live in a healthy way. Today it is an art to stay healthy, to eat healthy, to build up our life forces (instead of burning them up in stress and burnout), to relax and recover properly (without drugs), to sleep well (without sleeping pills), to be in balance (without antidepressants),

to master the soul forces (without psychotropic drugs), to overcome addictions, to be happy and content (without wanting to have more and more), to be able to love and have an open heart, to raise children, to deal joyfully with oneself and with others. The teachers, doctors, therapists and farmers who work out of Anthroposophy have an important task here to strengthen the consciousness of our humanity, as Rudolf Steiner described anthroposophy, and to develop it further in practical life.

2. Soul development. Here a renewed branch work could play an important role. Its purpose is not only to read texts together in order to get to know Anthroposophy, but also to promote awakening "on" the soul of the other, to support the transformation of the members' soul forces, to connect the participants in the group work in a culture of encounter, to understand and order the old karma, and to awaken the members' initiatives. To accompany this work, people with psychological and conversational skills are needed.

3. Spiritual development. Free forms of work in the School for Spiritual Science could give new impulses here, in freely held class lessons and in the common work in the Sections. This should be accompanied by people who have conscious experiences in the spiritual world, who can do spiritual research and who can advise others in their meditations and on their path of initiation.

4. The work on a new culture. This is the work in initiatives in the world that is done by Michaelites. They should be able to build islands of culture and mystery centers where they work. This happens on a small scale in the initiatives that already exist. The Anthroposophical Social Impulse should provide the basis for all the work.

The youth need their own circles. They want to go their own ways in developing self-awareness and in discovering the world. Here lies the future of Anthroposophy. It challenges us to develop a new awareness of our life goals, our identity, our inner work, meditation and training paths, our destiny, how we deal with the powers of our double and their transformation, how we deal with technology and the problems of our time. Many young people are looking for a conscious way of life and new educational paths. These are the themes of a new Anthroposophy.

A comparison of the structure of the Anthroposophical Society with the social form of the School of the White Brotherhood founded in Bulgaria by Rudolf Steiner's contemporary and spiritual brother Peter Deunov (1864-1944) may support the need for decentralization. According to Deunov, the White Brotherhood (or White Lodge) exists in the spiritual world under the leadership of Christ. The Michael School, which Rudolf Steiner brought to earth, can be seen as part of it. Deunov founded a spiritual community in 1900, not an association with members, but a brotherhood with many thousands of followers. In 1922 he opened an occult school with two classes. The first class was open to everyone, the second class was for selected young people. Also a secret circle (the Inner School) existed the most advanced students. After his death this occult school was not continued.

After the disappearance of communism, the White Brotherhood was registered as a community in 1990. The local member groups are autonomous, decide for themselves what they do and choose their leader. The School of the White Brotherhood has no members and is open to everyone. It teaches a spiritual path that is focused on Love, Wisdom and Truth. The community has a board that creates conditions for the work of these groups and connects them with each other. There are committees for the work areas. All lecture cycles, including the occult, are freely accessible and for sale in most bookshops in Bulgaria.

## 6. A Model for the Future

For a century we have been at a turning point in the development of culture and society. This development is no longer based on the social elite, which has become entangled in materialism, its power and its economic interests. New developments must now be based on individuals who connect with each other in communities.

In ancient societies, initiates who received inspiration from the spiritual world gave guidance to culture. That has long since ceased to be the case. According to Rudolf Steiner, since the 20th century the principle of initiation can once again become a principle of our civilization. Although there are strong forces in our materialistic culture that want to prevent this, the connection with our higher I can open the way to initiation for everyone. This is possible through the awakening of the spirit as a result of inner development and encounters with others. This creates the possibility of a conscious connection with the spiritual world, from which we can receive inspiration. With these inspirations we can work in small communities on the renewal of our culture and on a conscious and spiritual way of life.

Every community can contribute to this. This has three aspects: a social aspect (the members go through a social process with each other), a spiritual aspect (the connection with the source of inspiration) and a practical aspect (the work in an initiative). The spiritual aspect connects us with the spiritual world and with spiritual beings, with the spiritual (Anthroposophical) movement in the spiritual world. In the practical aspect we become part of the spiritual (Anthroposophical) movement on earth. The social aspect brings us into a process of community building, which, through the social impulse described in this book, is given a spiritual purpose.

Just as each community stands in its own way in the social life between heaven and earth, so Rudolf Steiner wanted to build a threefold, differentiated structure within which large groups of people could develop into initiators within this polarity of the spiritual and the earthly world. This Society should be a model for this development and be able to unite people in order to do this in harmony with each other. It is a model that prepares the social life of the next (Slavic) cultural epoch. This was Steiner's innovative vision of a threefold Society as a germ community of the future.

In the School of Spiritual Science the connection with the spiritual world had to be opened up so that new mysteries could take place and spiritual research could be coordinated. In the Anthroposophical Society (as renewed at the conference of Christmas 1923-24), people could meet on the social level, have spirit awakening conversations, develop their soul life, and come to initiatives together. Initiatives are taken from a possibly shared karmic past or to form new karma. The General Anthroposophical Society should support the work in the School of Spiritual Science, the member groups and the Anthroposophical spheres of work by creating good conditions and connecting the initiatives.

Different competences were required for each of these three sections, which were united in Rudolf Steiner. After Steiner's death this functional division was lost and a unitary structure was created in which the three sections could no longer function properly. This calls for an unbundling of the present structure so that an autonomous School of Spiritual Science, a federation of autonomous member groups and a supporting society can be created. The diagram below shows Rudolf Steiner's threefold concept.

> **Spiritual movement in the spiritual world**
> (source of inspiration for cultural innovation)
>
> Three aspects of cultural renewal:
>
> **1. Opening up to inspirations from the spiritual world**
> (School of Spiritual Science)
>
> **2. Connecting people to take initiatives**
> (Anthroposophical Society, now in the etheric world)
>
> **3. Creating conditions for the initiatives**
> (task of the General Anthroposophical Society)
>
> **Spiritual movement on earth**
> (arises from questions of our time and lives in initiatives)

When a group of people work on the questions of our time from shared ideals and spiritual visions, also outside official Anthroposophy, these three aspects become visible. In their conversations they enter into a process of community formation. Spiritually, we can connect this aspect with the Anthroposophical Society of the Christmas Conference, which, as described in this book, no longer exists in earthly form since 1925 (no. 2 in the diagram). The members of this group study the relevant literature and get to know each other. A small community is thus formed, at the level of the soul, in the exchange from person to person, in which the spirit, the individual Self, is awakened. This happens by asking each other questions and in the search for possibilities to do something together in the world around us, to take an initiative. It is not important how big this is.

In an initiative they work on an aspect of cultural renewal that is important for themselves and their environment. This can be an educational task in one's own family, care for one's fellow humans, a reading or study group, a working group, a therapeutic initiative, a spiritual center, a publishing house, an institute, a farm, a school, a medical practice. In this way they become part of the spiritual (Anthroposophical) movement on earth. This leads to an ongoing and sometimes difficult process of inner transformation and cooperation, with each other and with the people for whom the initiative is important.

The bearers of an initiative need inspiration for it. This is the second aspect, making a connection with the spiritual world, i.e. with helping spiritual beings. This connection with the spiritual (Anthroposophical) movement in the spiritual world develops through study, training and meditation, and a form of conversation called the "cult of knowledge cult" in this book. This is how the group enters the field of the School of Spiritual Science (no. 1 in the diagram). Through the inspiration and insights received by the group from spiritual beings, the initiative can become an incipient mystery center connected to the spiritual world.

Developing an new field of activities requires a third aspect of creating conditions for the initiatives, guidance, support and connecting initiatives with each other. This "etheric organizing" can take place in many ways. In the Anthroposophical world this is the task of the General Anthroposophical Society (no. 3 in the diagram).

In this way Anthroposophy opens up a path of innovative community formation and can be a help to all those who wish to share responsibility for the future of mankind. If the resulting initiatives work on the basis of Anthroposophy's social impulse, the society of the future will emerge in these communities.

This chapter described the steps of the Social Impulse of Anthroposophy that can lead to the formation of new communities.

Anthroposophical initiatives on this path of community formation can transform into cultural islands, where people in the new mysteries consciously cross the threshold of the spiritual world and support one another in doing so. This is where Anthroposophy is born again. The spirit now works in individuals, no longer from institutions. The General Anthroposophical Society can fulfil a helping and supporting function in this process, which is based on individual people and their inner connection with the being Anthropo-Sophia.

The Anthroposophical Society, founded at the Christmas Conference of 1923-24 and disappeared from the consciousness of the members in 1925, lives on in the etheric world and includes people who have connected with the being Anthropo-Sophia. There is no need to re-establish this Society, as its members are already working together in a spiritual community and taking initiatives together. In a similar way, a Christian in a spiritual sense is not someone who is a member of an outer church, but someone who is internally connected to Christ. The church of primeval Christianity has also disappeared due to a lack of consciousness and lives in the spiritual world as the mystical body of Christ. This is the 'invisible church' whose members can meet in the visible church. It is the same with Anthropo-Sophia and her spiritual body, the Anthroposophical Society in the etheric world.

In several countries member groups have become increasingly autonomous in their activities. There are independent circles that read the class lessons and this leads to the question whether everything connected with the School for Spiritual Science cannot be organized independently by people who are committed to the work of Anthroposophy in the world. The General Anthroposophical Society can then create the necessary conditions for the work of its member groups and the School for Spiritual Science, and connect initiatives with each other, as was already foreseen in 1925 when it was established as an umbrella organization connecting the institutions that existed at that time (the clinic, the publishing house and the administrations of the spiritual Society and the Goetheanum building).

With this structure of a threefold Anthroposophical Society, the problem of the two Societies (the spiritual and the administrative) has been solved. This is a social form that suits modern times, in which people take initiatives with each other that are no longer judged from above but are supported and connected with initiatives of others. This is the social art of the future, with which we are already practicing the learning process of building in the "social etheric" space, with the help of the Social Impulse of Anthroposophy and the social skills of the participants.

As the work in the member groups, class circles, initiatives and sections becomes more self-organized, the board of the General Anthroposophical Society gets more room for its actual task, which is to support the initiatives of people who work from an anthroposophical impulse. They form the community of initiatives which stands in the tradition of the Christmas Conference of 1923-24 and which needs new impulses after a century. This renewal includes elements which the Anthroposophical movement has been working on for several decades and which can give concrete form to these new impulses. In this way, the spirit of this Christmas Conference is rekindled:

1. A contemporary presentation of anthroposophical points of view in society, to help people develop a new art of living and become familiar with these spiritual visions.
2. A new animation of the work in the member groups, so that people interested in Anthroposophy can get to know it, get to know themselves and each other, and discover how Anthroposophy may provide answers to the questions

of our time. This is the care of the life of the soul, in people and in society.

3. Working on the spiritual development of people and discovering new insights in the cooperation between them. For this purpose the method of the spiritual conversation (the "knowledge cult") is available. There are individual meditations and class lessons for sensitizing our inner perception and for developing higher forms of consciousness.
4. Discovering the new possibilities of communication with the spiritual world created by the development of the consciousness soul. These are the new mysteries, which are already a reality on a small scale.
5. Applying the Anthroposophical Social Impulse. This unites people in the groups and initiatives in which they explore the communities of the future. Their starting point is the search for solutions to the small and big issues of our time. In these communities they can receive inspiration from the spiritual world. They are guided in this by the spiritual being connecting with their work.
6. Creating cultural islands that arise from these initiatives, so that the new spirituality can radiate to a larger environment and connect people for whom the initiatives are important.
7. Making connections with other groups that work with Michaelic inspirations.

## EPILOGUE: AWAKENING TO A NEW ERA

Since the second half of the 19th century many events have taken place in spiritual life that we have yet to grasp in consciousness. Humanity has unconsciously crossed over the threshold to the spiritual world. Michael's era began in 1879, in 1899 the Kali Yuga (the Dark Age) expired and the new Age of Light, where the spiritual world wants to inspire people again, has begun. Anthroposophy is its first fruit, preparing us to meet the reappearing Christ in the etheric and opening in the new mysteries the way to the sphere of the Holy Spirit. They were inaugurated at the founding of the Anthroposophical Society at the Christmas Conference of 1923.

In the almost 100 years that have since passed, many people acquired a presentiment of the social world as mystery center, where the spirit wants to unite people for a new Whitsun festival to take place in human souls. It will come true once we take the double path of community building: that means when we broaden consciousness in group work and develop new social forces in meetings and cooperation. The processes of community building have only begun, and we are discovering know what kind of cultivation of soul and what kind of social forms are needed. We cannot reproach someone who is still caught in old structures of soul and social life. We all have our own pace. We know though, that opposing forces act through outdated social structures and frames of mind. This is why a clear consciousness is presently indispensable.

In this book some fundamental characteristics of the new mysteries were defined that are true for the new era as well. They relate to freeing the human individuality from fetters of authority and tradition. Spirituality must have a practical meaning for social life, right down to handling money. People are looking for real meetings to learn about others and themselves, and to awaken. New social forms of cooperation and living together are needed to provide a living sphere of rights; then, conscious karmic connections develop between people for new communities to arise. This is irradiated by the intimate closeness of Christ, who appears as inner teacher and helper, comforter and advisor, and gives everything we ask of Him in this sense.

Modern people can bring their forces of cognition, courage, morality and their heart to development in the new era. Then they become Michaelites. All these forces allow light to shine in the spiritual battles of our time. Rudolf Steiner saw the darkening of culture that began in 1933, and he hoped that the Anthroposophical movement would be strong enough to rescue European culture. That same year would witness Christ's new revelation in the etheric and the first repetition of the 33-year rhythm since the beginning of the new era of light. It was then that Nazism crossed this rhythm.

The second repetition occurred in the 1960s. Many people opened to the spiritual world and a new sense of life developed. Individual freedom, originality, free behavior, personal responsibility, openness to new experiences, radical criticism of materialistic society and hope for a culture of brotherhood became central values. This new culture is often called the New Age or the culture of Aquarius. We are not there yet. The astrological Age of Aquarius will only start in 2375 and the Slavic culture in 3574. Anthroposophy and the Bulgarian School of the White Brotherhood want to prepare this new culture, without falling into the illusion that we already live in a culture of love and brotherhood. The New Age is the age of the returning Christ.

At the end of the 20th century the 33-year rhythm appeared for the third time. By means of modern technology the opposing forces try to divert the forces of light and to lock people up in a consciousness prison. This is connected with the year 1998 (3 x 666), that represents the third return of the impulse of Gondishapur that started to work in the 7th century. It is an impulse coming from the Sun demon that intends to destroy the human I. The second return of this impulse (2 x 666 = 1332) can be connected with the destruction of the Order of the Knights Templar and the use of torture to conjure frightful images from the depth of the subconsciousness of the knights. Moreover, Steiner predicted the incarnation of the Prince of Darkness, Ahriman, at the very beginning of the 21st century. This incarnation is yet to appear, but its shadow is already noticeable everywhere. We live in an apocalyptic time, in which inner work and presence of mind are urgently necessary. In modern society a war is waged against the spirituality that Anthroposophy represents.

Steiner spoke in apocalyptic images about the year 1933,[102] the end of the 20th century and the time immediately following. On September 20, 1924, he warned that "before the etheric Christ can be understood rightly, mankind must cope with meeting the Beast that will rise from the abyss in 1933." And shortly before, on July 19, 1924, he said:

> In the course of this century, when the first century after the end of Kali Yuga has passed, humanity will stand either at the grave of all civilization or at the beginning of the era in which the battle of Michael will be fought in favor of the Michael im-

---

102  Rudolf Steiner: *Apokalypse und Priesterwirken* (1924), Dornach 1995 (CW 346).

pulse in the souls of men, uniting intelligence with spirituality in their hearts.[103]

The survival and further development of Michaelic spirituality, expressed in an initial, imperfect form in Anthroposophy, is at stake. The apocalyptic Beast from the abyss wants to destroy this spirituality and already inspired the self-destruction of the Anthroposophical Society in 1935. This touches the self-consciousness of the Anthroposophical movement that was so darkened in the 1930s. The 1960s brought a first awakening by spiritual impulses passing through the whole world. Since the turn of the century this self-consciousness has to awaken even more so that free people can unite and create a new spiritual culture.

Starting-point for a renewal of Anthroposophy is the care for the soul. We are all presently more or less ill in our soul, Anthroposophists included. We need forms of group work that heal through artistic activities and the art of conversation, where people can open up to themselves and others and unite: forms that include advice on paths of schooling, exercises and mutual help on the basis of soul friendship.

The development of soul has individual and social paths. Male and female, head and heart, can unite in each human being when we follow both paths. Development includes the path of individually broadening consciousness as well as the social path of the Anthroposophical Social Impulse. Developing the soul leads to awakening a new, inner person, to opening the heart, and to community building. Then research that belongs to the new mysteries can focus on addressing current issues and offering insight into the activity of opposing forces in the world. This research must also be open to constructive aspects in other spiritual and social streams.

---

103 Rudolf Steiner: *Karmic Relationships*, Vol. 6 (1924), London 1975 (CW 240).

The spiritual world wants to inspire humanity anew. Not in order to jump to the next cultural epoch, but really grow into the tasks of our present culture and then find the way into the next one in ourselves. We must unite with the earth, understand the hidden nooks and crannies of our soul and place them in the light of consciousness to develop and transform our personality. Then spiritual and social forces will grow as well. We will be able to touch the sphere of the Holy Spirit in conversations and common paths of research and open to the inspirations of the spiritual world.

We are only at the beginning and forces from the past are not yet overcome; they hinder awakening to the new era. The hierarchical Roman spirit and intellectualism, still active in spiritual life and in Anthroposophical work, must be overcome socially and spiritually for spiritual life to advance into the new century. In face of the looming disappearance of culture, it is time to ignite a new Whitsun fire in our soul to pass through the world, awaken people spiritually and found a culture of the heart. The hope of millions of people turns to a new Anthroposophy that is appropriate to the times to lead the way. We are faced with the task of freeing Anthroposophy from the tomb of social and spiritual forms that belong to an old era so that Anthroposophy can become a resurrecting force in human beings who feel responsible for what takes place in the world. But we should also know that Anthroposophy is already living in the higher consciousness of humanity.